MODERN EMBROIDERY

MODERN EMBROIDERY

A Book of Stitches
to Unleash Creativity

RACHAEL DOBBINS

yellow pear 🍐 press

CORAL GABLES

For permission requests, please contact the publisher at:
Mango Publishing Group
2850 S Douglas Road, 4th Floor
Coral Gables, FL 33134 USA
info@mango.bz

For special orders, quantity sales, course adoptions and corporate sales, please email the publisher at sales@mango.bz. For trade and wholesale sales, please contact Ingram Publisher Services at customer.service@ingramcontent.com or +1.800.509.4887.

Modern Embroidery: A Book of Stitches to Unleash Creativity

Library of Congress Cataloging-in-Publication number: 2022943070
ISBN: (p) 978-1-68481-009-3 (e) 978-1-68481-010-9
BISAC category code CRA044000, CRAFTS & HOBBIES / Needlework / Cross-Stitch

Printed in the United States of America

To my little girl, Darla, my forever inspiration.
A strong-minded, independent little person.
I love seeing the world through her eyes.

TABLE OF CONTENTS

INTRODUCTION

"Talent is a pursued interest. Anything that you're willing to practice, you can do."

—Bob Ross, American painter

I've always known that I wanted to be an artist. I've drawn and painted for as long as I can remember. After studying fine art, then falling into textiles, I discovered my love for embroidery. While I was at university, I was encouraged to think outside the box with my embroidery—to create texture and layer my stitches in the same way I was taught to layer paint. I wanted to create something unconventional with simple materials, rather than sticking to traditional techniques. When I started embroidering again after taking some time off, it was a no-brainer for me to follow that advice: not to overthink the stitches and the traditional techniques, but to let my fingers stitch. I now like to mix both media I've grown to love: embroidery and painting.

After throwing out the rule book and stitching more freely, I would look at the subject matter and ask myself what stitch I would use to make it look realistic and create a lot of texture. What would convey the idea of leaves in a tree, or, how could I fill in a section to create movement in a wave? Embroidery started becoming an interpretation, something where the possibilities were endless. Letting my mind run freely, I started letting the threads hang from the embroidery, rather than being confined to the hoop. I started knotting the threads and making mini macramé hangers, cutting the threads and creating three-dimensional fringe flowers, or manipulating the threads to hang and resemble hair.

I describe my embroidery pieces as Expressionist paintings—thread paintings, if you will—and I've been pushing them into the art category, especially when it comes to land and seascapes. I hope this book will open your eyes to the possibilities of embroidery. Remember, there is no right or wrong way to stitch.

"You have unlimited power. You have the ability to move mountains. You can bend rivers."

—Bob Ross

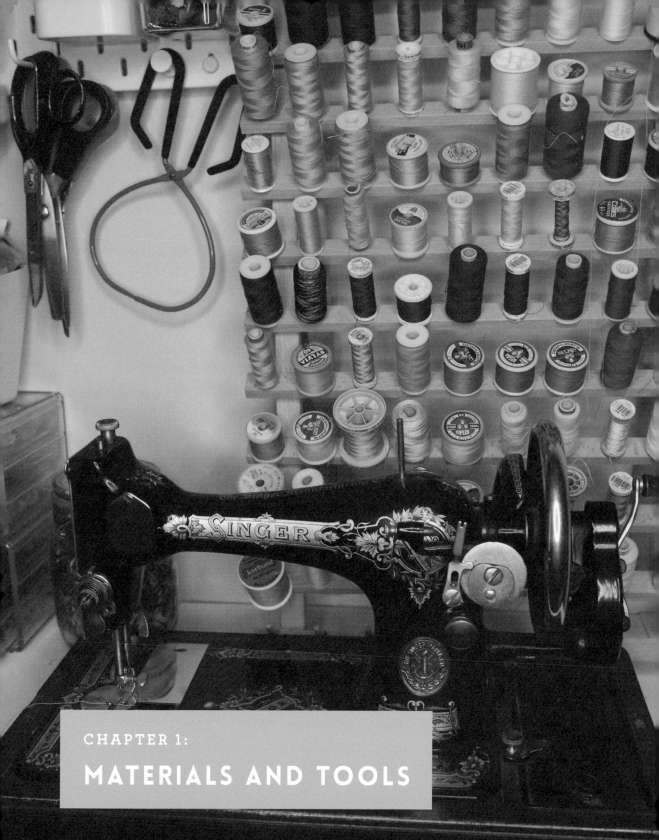

CHAPTER 1:

MATERIALS AND TOOLS

If you already love to embroider, you may have many of these items in your sewing box. If you are new to the craft, this comprehensive list will be more than you need to begin, but it will give you a good idea of all the fabulous tools available. Not everything on this list is necessary to start these projects. The main items you need are a needle, an embroidery hoop, a handful of cotton embroidery threads, and a piece of fabric. The stitching key and the colours I suggest you use are just that: *suggestions*. Freedom and creativity are always encouraged.

THREADS

Stranded cotton embroidery thread is the most commonly used thread. It comes in six divisible strands that allow you to play with the weight of your stitches, to add fine lines or depth to your work. And it comes in a wide range of colours, which allow embroiderers to let their creativity flow.

NEEDLES

Needles range in length, thickness, eye size, and sharpness. You can never have enough needles, in my opinion, but it's important to pick a suitable needle for the type of fabric and threads you are using. There is no rule about what size needle to use with any particular embroidery thread; it's just trial and error, as well as personal preference. If it's difficult to pull the needle through the fabric, then try a thicker needle. Alternatively, if the needle leaves a visible hole in the fabric, you might need a sharper or thinner needle. When choosing a needle, note that the higher the number indicating the needle size, the finer the needle.

Embroidery/Crewel Needle

A crewel needle is a medium-length needle with a long eye and sharp point. It works well as an all-around embroidery needle that will be perfect for most any technique or surface. The sharp tip is ideal for piercing tightly woven fabric without leaving visible holes.

Tapestry Needle

A tapestry needle is a medium-length needle with a large eye and blunt point. They work best on woven fabrics such as cotton and heavy (upholstery) linen, or any fabric that doesn't need a hole made. I use these for my thread-painted embroideries when the fabric isn't a tight weave, in sizes 20, 22, and 24.

Chenille Needle

A chenille needle is sharp with a long eye. Size 22 is great on most fabrics. The large, long eye is used to accommodate your thread, and the point keeps the fabric intact when pierced. I also find chenille to be a good choice when stitching with metallic threads.

Milliners Needle

A milliners needle is sharp, with a small eye that's the same thickness as the needle, so the eye doesn't bulge at the top. It's also known as a straw needle. The longest on the list, it is perfect for creating bullion knots and cast-on stitches, which require a lot of thread on the needle before being inserted into the fabric.

Quilting Needle

Also known as *betweens*, these needles have a small, rounder eye; they are short and have a short point, which makes them perfect for fine stitches. Quilting needles are used for detailed handwork, tailoring, and quilt making. I use these needles when I'm hand-stitching dolls together because they don't mark the fabric, cause it to fray, or make large holes.

FABRIC

Embroidery can be done on almost any type of fabric: the possibilities are endless. My "go-to" fabric is anything that is woven. It's a good choice to embroider on because woven fabrics hold their shape inside the hoop. They won't pucker or pull, and can handle heavy amounts of embroidery, if you go for a thicker weight of woven fabric. There is a huge variety of woven fabrics, from denim to cheesecloth, canvas to lawn.

Canvas

Canvas is a plain-woven fabric, typically made from cotton and linen. The texture of canvas is slightly rough to the touch, and it is known for being durable and sturdy. It's perfect to use when you're adding a lot of embroidery, stitching a lot of surface area, or adding lots of texture.

Cotton Twill

Twill has a diagonal rib pattern with a distinct darker front side and a lighter back side. It has a high thread count, which means the fabric is opaque, thick, and durable.

Poplin

Poplin is a plain-woven cotton fabric with fine horizontal ribs, which makes the fabric strong. Poplin has a slightly silky surface. It's the perfect fabric for doll making.

TOOLS TO TRANSFER PATTERNS ONTO FABRIC

Transferring your design onto fabric can be tricky. There is no right or wrong way to do this, and there are several options available. My one rule with this is, if you're going to cover the whole hoop with embroidery, you can use absolutely anything, because it doesn't matter if marks are left on the fabric. With something that is going to have fabric exposed, you need something that will disappear after the project is complete.

Heat Pens

Heat pens work on most fabrics, and they feel like a regular pen. Once you've finished your project, these pens' marks vanish under a heat gun or an iron. It's always advised to test the fabric first because they do leave white marks on darker fabrics.

Pencil

A standard pencil can be used for marking fabric. As long as you use them lightly, their marks are easily erased or washed away.

Chalk

Marking chalk is something you can use with darker fabrics. Note, though, that it rubs away, so it's not the best option for something that's going to be handled for long periods of time.

Water-Soluble Fabric

This is my pattern transfer "go-to" option. There are two types I use: an opaque, plastic-like fabric, and a thin white fabric. The white water-soluble "fabric" can come with an adhesive backing; this form is named Magic Paper. These options make it easy to lay over the template to transfer. Make sure you don't use a pen that can bleed into your work, however, as the soluble fabric needs to be washed away after the embroidery is complete. Most of the time, I can just pull the soluble fabric away from my work, if I've made a lot of holes by embroidering.

Carbon Transfer Paper

Designs can be transferred using this paper unless the fabric is thick. It's easy to place over the template and trace on, and then go back over the lines once you've placed it over the fabric. It can be washed away, but I do tend to make sure my stitching covers the lines it leaves.

OTHER HELPFUL SUPPLIES

Embroidery Hoop

An embroidery hoop is essential. It holds your fabric taut while you work, keeping the fabric from puckering and your stitches from pulling the fabric. A lot of my thread-painted landscapes need to be kept in the hoops when complete because, depending on the length of the stitch, the threads can become loose when the project is taken out. Hoops come in different sizes and styles, from wooden to the faux-wood-grain effect, such as "flexi hoops." I like to use a hoop with every project, whether I'm creating "hoop art" (something that will stay in the hoop and be placed on my wall) or stitching on clothing and then removing the hoop. Hoops keep projects neat, tidy, and easily workable.

Embroidery Scissors

Although these aren't essential, I do find embroidery scissors helpful. They are compact and their points are thin and sharp, which makes it easy to cut the threads close to the fabric. But truly, any scissors will do the job.

Pinking Shears

Zigzag scissors are not essential but can be used as an added precaution for seams. They stop fabrics from fraying.

DOLL-MAKING SUPPLIES

Doll making requires a few special supplies. I use a sewing machine to stitch the body, legs, and arms together, but if you don't have access to one, you can hand-stitch them just as effectively.

Thread

You'll need either cotton or polyester thread on a bobbin. Both are strong threads, made to cope with highly stressed seams, and have a high breaking point. They are suitable for both machine and hand embroidery.

Toy Stuffing

You'll need stuffing material to fill your doll, to give it shape and form. It should be smooth and completely filled so it doesn't become lumpy and uneven. The two popular types of filling are polyester fiber and wool. Like anything, you'll get better at stuffing dolls with practice. The key is to add small amounts at a time and press enough into the arms and legs so they aren't droopy or too empty.

Turning Tool

Turning tools are a must-have when it comes to creating the doll's arms and legs. They allow you to quickly and easily turn the fabric back to right-side-out. When the doll has been sewn, it will be inside-out at first. The turning tool, which is basically a tube, can be inserted to gently push the fabric back to right-side-out.

CHAPTER 2:

STITCH GUIDE

STITCHING TECHNIQUES

Many embroidery stitches are used in this book. Below is a list, with tutorials for those needed to complete the projects.

Bullion Knot

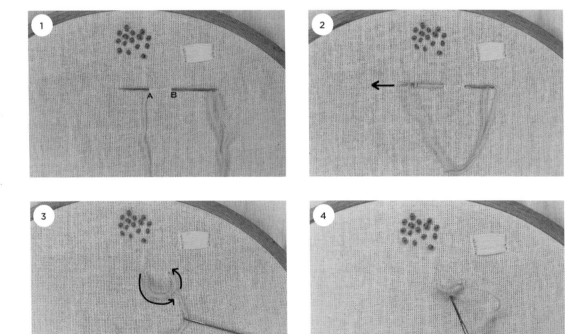

1.   Bullion knot Point A to B.
2.   Wrap the floss around the needle and pull the needle through.
3.   Pull the knot to the fabric and place the needle through the hole.
4.   Secure knot to fabric (optional).

This is an elongated knot that adds thick texture. It's best embroidered with a milliners needle with an eye that is the same thickness as the needle. Begin by piercing through the fabric at Point A; go into the fabric at Point B and then back over to Point A, without pulling the thread through the fabric. Push the needle back to Point A, leaving roughly a third of the needle in the fabric. Start to wrap the thread around the needle, over and around, keeping hold of the thread to maintain tension. Pull the needle through the wraps of thread until all the thread is pulled to the front and the bullion knots sit at the surface of the fabric. Then push the needle back through the original hole at Point B.

Bullion-Knot-Stitched Rose

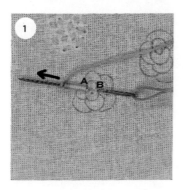 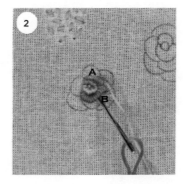 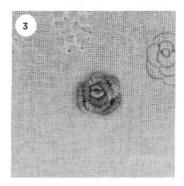

1. Bullion knot, how to layer each stitch to create petals.
2. Each section is stitched from Point A to B.
3. Bullion-knot rose.

The beauty of this stitch is that it's not always the same; each rose turns out different. It all just adds to the beauty of a rose and how unique each one is in real life. Each petal edge is the start and end of the bullion knot, marked A and B. Start at the centre of the rose and work around until you get to the outer petals. The petals in the middle are smaller and only need a few wraps of floss on the needle. The larger outer petals need double the amount.

Cast-On Stitch

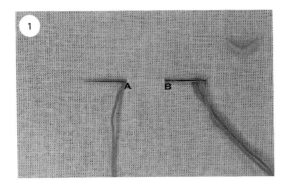

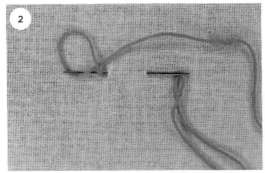

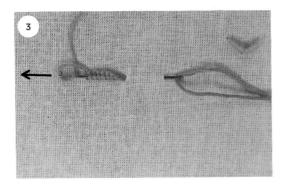

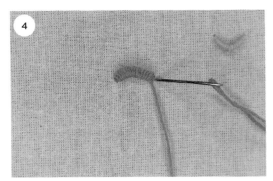

1. Cast-On Stitch A to B.
2. Direction of twist onto needle.
3. Twists added to needle and pull needle out.

4. Pull stitch tight to fabric and push needle into hole.

This is a long-knotted stitch that is built up on the needle like a bullion knot. It is a three-dimensional stitch that stands up from the fabric, which can easily be shaped to your project. To start, come up through the fabric at Point A and stitch over to Point B, not pulling the thread through. Come back up through the fabric in the same hole as Point A, but don't pull the needle all the way through the fabric, just the tip. Take your index finger and twist the thread and loop it onto the needle. Start to wrap the floss arrowed in the diagram around the needle with a twisting motion. You are casting the thread to the needle, so add as many twists as you need. Once you're finished, push the needle back into the Point B hole and pull the thread tight.

Double Cast-On Stitch

A DOUBLE CAST-ON STITCH
IS THE SAME AS ON THE
PREVIOUS PAGE, BUT,
INSTEAD OF TWISTING THE
FLOSS ONTO THE NEEDLE,
YOU NEED TO DOUBLE OVER
THE THREAD AND TWIST
EACH STRAND ALTERNATELY
ONTO THE NEEDLE.

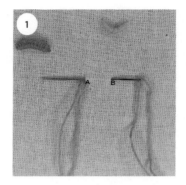
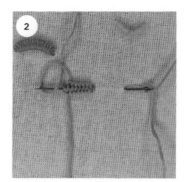
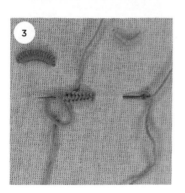
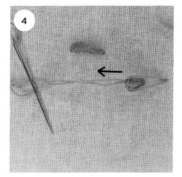
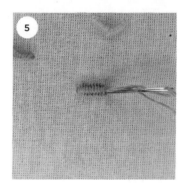

1. Double Cast-On Stitch Point A to B.
2. Twist top thread onto needle.
3. Twist bottom thread onto needle.
4. Pull needle out.
5. Secure stitch by going back into fabric.

A double cast-on stitch is the same as on the previous page but, instead of twisting the floss onto the needle, you need to double over the thread and twist each strand alternately onto the needle.

To start, come up through the fabric at Point A and stitch over to Point B, not pulling the thread through. Come back up through the fabric in the same hole as Point A, but don't pull the needle all the way through the fabric, just the tip. With your index finger, twist one of the threads and loop it onto the needle, then do the same with the other one. Keep building up the twists. Once you're finished, push the needle back into Point B hole and pull the thread tight.

Cast-On-Stitched Rose

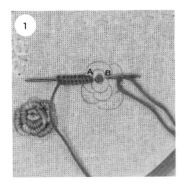
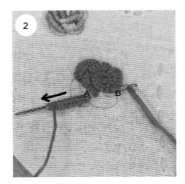

1. Cast-on stitch, from A to B, twist floss onto needle.
2. Each section is a separate cast-on stitch.
3. The cast-on stitches are shaped the same as the drawing.

The cast-on rose works the same as the bullion-knot rose. Add a cast-on stitch to each petal shape to build up the rose. The number of times you twist the floss onto the needle determines how three-dimensional the stitch will become.

Chain Stitch

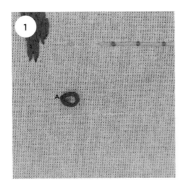
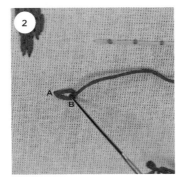
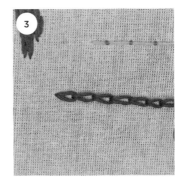

1. Stitch loop at Point A.
2. Stitch another loop at Point B.

3. Repeat.

Come through the fabric at Point A and go straight back through at the same point, leaving a little loop as you pull the thread through the fabric. At the edge of the loop, at Point B, come through the fabric to secure that loop and then go back through the same hole, leaving a small loop, and repeat.

Couch Stitch

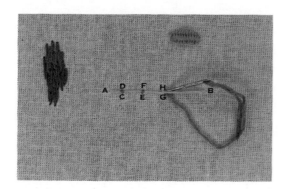

Anchor the thread and come through the fabric at Point A, then stitch over to Point B. Keep the thread tight to the fabric. Tack the long stitch down with tiny vertical stitches. Come through fabric at Point C to D, E to F, and so on.

French Knot

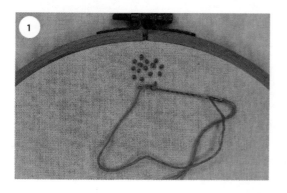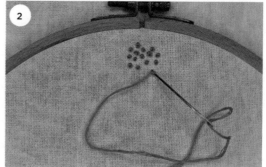

1.   French knot: Wrap the floss over the needle.
2.   Go back into the same hole.

Once you've mastered this knot, it's one of the easiest stitches to use. It's a perfect stitch to create texture and works well for the centres of flowers—definitely a go-to stitch of mine. The most important thing is to know that practice makes perfect, so if it doesn't go smoothly at first, don't worry. Keep working on it, and soon you will be able to create beautiful French knots. The needle you choose should have an eye that's the same size as the width of the needle. If the eye is bigger than the body of the needle, it will be difficult to pass it through the wrapped thread and the fabric. Anchor your thread and pull it through the fabric. Place the needle on top of the fabric horizontally while still keeping hold of it. Wrap the floss over and around the needle one or two times, keeping the thread taut. Still keeping hold of the thread, push the needle through the fabric in the same hole you made at the start, and pull the thread through until the knot tightens up at the surface of the fabric.

Granitos

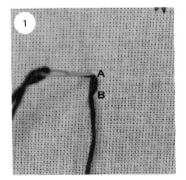 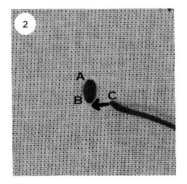 

1. Granitos stitch: Three stitches from A to B.
2. Granitos-stitched flower, repeat three stitches from C to B.
3. Granitos-stitched flower.

This is a chunky stitch that resembles a grain of rice; the idea is to layer straight stitches on top of each other. I love using this stitch for flower petals. The granitos stitch is comprised of a series of straight stitches using the same entry and exit point.

Start by embroidering a straight stitch between Point A and Point B. Follow with another stitch in the same exact points. When you pull the thread tight, the stitch should lie to the side of the first stitch. Add another stitch and lay it to the opposite side. You can finish the stitch here, or add a couple more to make it plumper.

Invisible Stitch or Slip Stitch

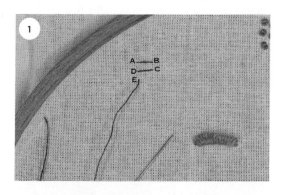

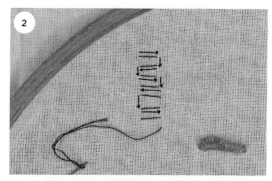

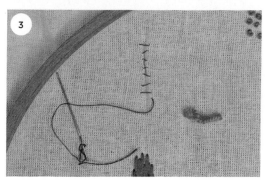

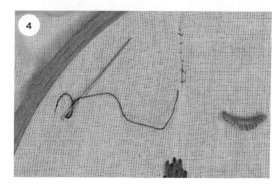

1. Invisible stitch from A to B to C.
2. Invisible stitch, direction of stitches.
3. Pulling stitches in.
4. Closing the gap.

To stitch two pieces of fabric together without visible stitches, use the slip stitch, with simple stitches that are strategically placed. Push the needle into the fabric at Point A and out at Point B. On the same side as Point B, come into the fabric at Point C. Go into the other side, exactly opposite, at Point D, then repeat. You'll create tiny little tacks that you can pull in tight once you reach the end of the opening you are closing.

Long and Short Stitches

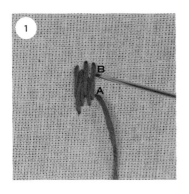 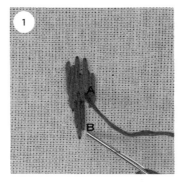 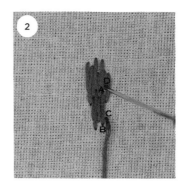

1. Long and short stitch from A to B.
2. Stitch from C to D.

This stitch is good for blending colours together, especially over large surface areas. There is no right or wrong way to do this. The name says everything; it's a mix of long and short stitches done close together, like a satin stitch. Come in through the fabric at Point A, and out at Point B. Begin the next stitch as close to Point B as possible (Point C) and finish the stitch at the length you desire, Point D, then repeat.

Running Stitch

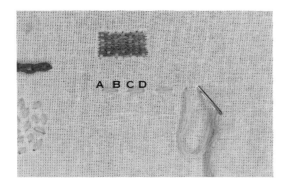

A running stitch is a loosely placed row of short stitches that are used to gather fabric, stitch basic hems, or hold fabric together. I use a running stitch to hand-embroider around a shape, to mark an area I want to stitch together on the sewing machine. Start at Point A, and stitch over to Point B. The next stitch will have the same width as this stitch. From B, go back into the fabric at Point C and then over to Point D. Then repeat.

Seed Stitch

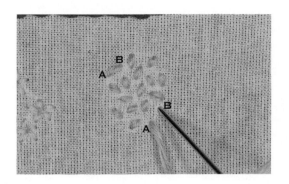

This stitch is an easy way to quickly add colour or texture. It's also sometimes good to use to fill in small spaces.

Anchor the thread to the fabric and start to add tiny stitches at random, from Point A to Point B.

Five-Point Star/Flower

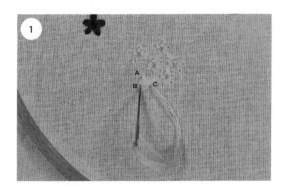
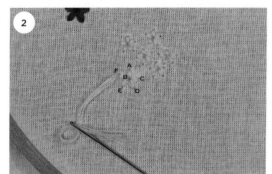

1. Five-point star/flower stitch from A to B, C to B.
2. D to B, E to B, F to B.

This stitch is a collection of tack-like stitches that join in the centre. The stitches can be made chunky by making five granitos stitches and joining them from the centre.

Start by embroidering a straight stitch from Point A to Point B, then coming back through the fabric at Point C and back through to Point B. Stitch from Point D to B, E to B, and then F to B.

Satin Stitch

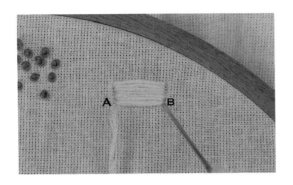

A satin stitch adds a smooth, seamless finish to your embroidery. The idea is to create a satin look, using long straight stitches that are close together to fill a space. The flatter you want your stitches to look, the fewer strands you should use. Again, this is a stitch that comes with practice. Begin by threading a needle and pulling it through the fabric where you want to begin. Consider that Point A. You will then lay the thread (or floss) across the top of the fabric to the point where you want the stitch to end. That is Point B. You will then repeat the process by adding the next stitch as close as possible to the previous stitch to fill the space. Pierce the fabric at Point A and go back through the fabric at Point B. Again, the next stitch should be as close to Point A as you can get, and back to Point B. Repeat the process until the area is covered.

Split Stitch

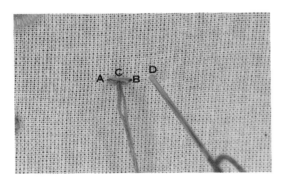

This stitch is used to outline and fill larger areas of embroidery. Unlike the satin or long and short stitches, the split stitch adds texture. Embroider a small stitch to the fabric from Point A to Point B, roughly the size of a grain of rice; come back through the fabric halfway through the original stitch (Point C) and back through the fabric at Point D, again making it roughly the size of a grain of rice, and repeat.

Stem Stitch

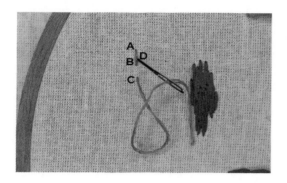

The stem stitch is used for outlining. It's a collection of straight stitches that overlap—perfect for crafting flowers or stitching stems. Anchor the thread into the fabric and stitch from Point A to Point B, then Point C to Point D

Weave or Basket Stitch

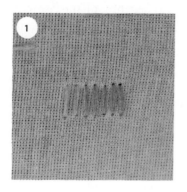

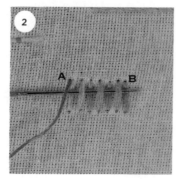

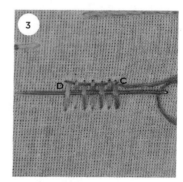

1.   Grid of straight stitches
2.   Weaving from Point A to B.

3.   Weaving from Point C to D.

Start by stitching long stitches in the area you want to fill, leaving spaces in between, sort of like a satin stitch but not so close together. Once you have created a vertical grid, come into the fabric at Point A and weave the thread under and over each long stitch, until you get to the end of the last stitch at Point B. Repeat, but in the opposite direction. If your last weave was over the long stitch, then you need to start under. Keep building up until the space is covered.

Whipped Back Stitch

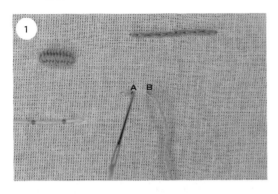

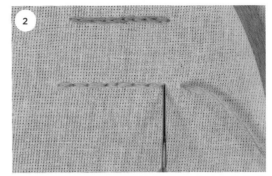

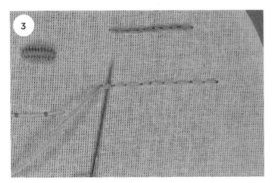

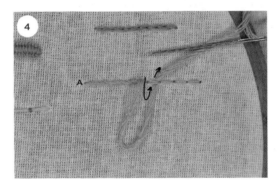

1. Back stitch, from Point A to B.
2. Back stitch.
3. Weave into the back stitch.
4. Direction of weave.

A whipped back stitch is perfect for outlines. It's very simple to do and works well.

For a back stitch, add a stitch to the fabric. Come through the same length as the original stitch from Point B and back into the fabric in the previous hole, Point A. The stitches will join together. Continue until you reach your desired length. To turn the back stitch into a whipped back stitch, come through the original hole at Point A and, instead of going in and out of the fabric, weave the thread along the stitches, over and under. To secure the thread, go into the fabric through one of the holes made by the back stitch.

CHAPTER 3:
THREAD PAINTINGS

LAVENDER FIELD

In this embroidery lesson, you only need three stitching techniques: French knot, satin stitch, and long and short stitches. This project allows you to play around with texture, building up your stitches to create form and depth. This will be a labour of love, because you need to be fond of French knots to create this landscape. The good news is that you will be a master of the French knot by the end of this project!

What You Need:

- Seven-inch embroidery hoop
- Cotton or linen fabric
- DMC thread: colours for the sky 519, 598, 827, 964, 3753

- DMC thread: colours for lavender 33, 371, 209, 210, 327, 553, 554, 3727, 3835, 3836, C554, E415, E3837

This embroidery is one of the easiest templates to transfer to fabric, with simple lines. I've used natural calico, as it is just thin enough to see the template through to trace but still sturdy enough that it holds its shape in the hoop, even when a lot of embroidery is added.

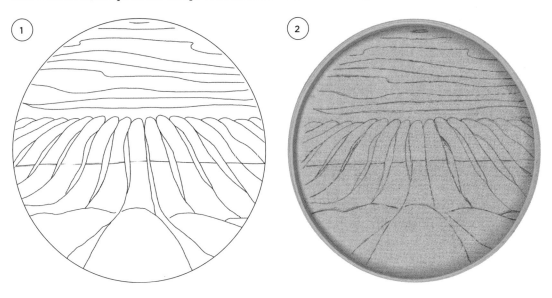

1. Template on page 172.

2. Transferred to fabric.

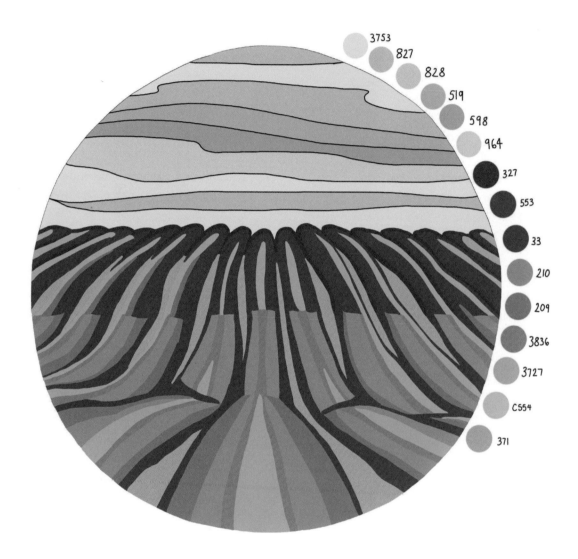

3753
827
828
519
598
964
327
553
33
210
209
3836
3727
C554
371

Sky

Let's begin with the simplest part of the scene. The sky is blocked into five shades of blue, from top to bottom. For each colour, split the floss into three strands. Use long and short stitches to fill in the sections. (Colour selection is noted below.)

Colour sequence for sky: 964, 827, 3753, 827, 519, 598, 964, 3753, 827, 3753

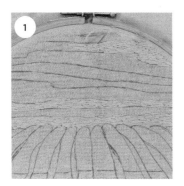 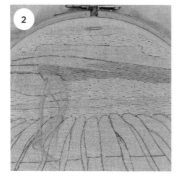 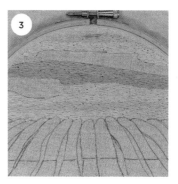

1.   Long and short stitches.
2.   Marking out the sky by adding sections of colours.
3.   Blocking sky.

Field

Start with the greenery between the lavender bushes, using Mustard colour 371. Satin-stitch between the clusters, using all six strands of floss and keeping the satin stitch in the same direction.

Using the colour chart for reference, French-knot along the end of the field; along the horizon, where the field meets the sky, work in Dark Violet colour 327. You want to French-knot onto the line.

French-knot in front of each line you've just stitched with Fuchsia colour 33 (this should sit in front of colour 327). Then continue along the outlines until the shape of the field is filled in.

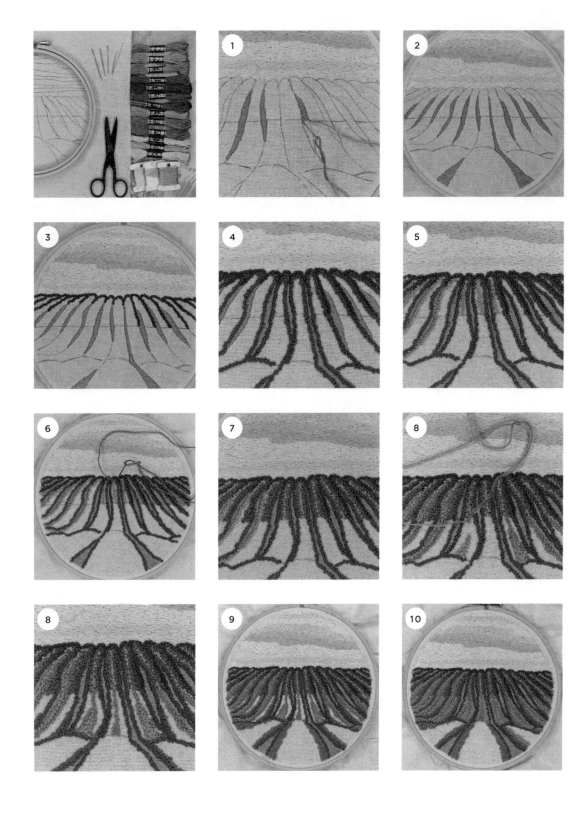

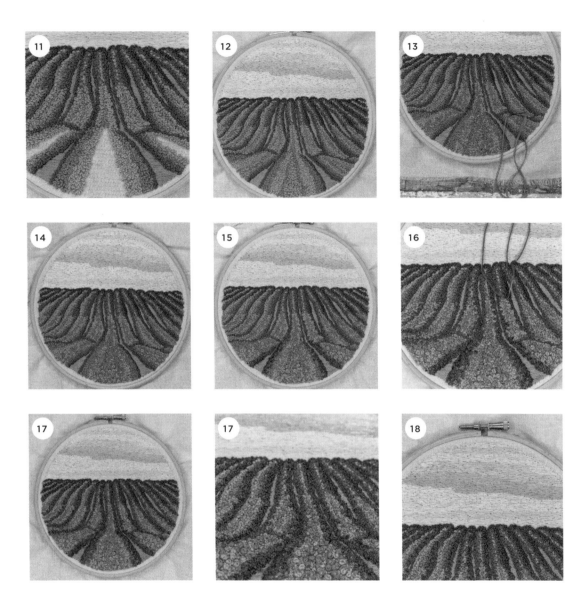

1. Adding greenery.
2. Satin-stitched sections.
3. Horizon in 327.
4. Outline the rest of the field in 33.
5. Highlight in 3727.
6. Filling in with 553.
7. Blending colours together with 209.
8. Adding highlight with 3727 and 3836.
9. Sections of 209.
10. Fill in with 210.
11. Colours 209 and 210 together, creating a triangle shape left to fill.

12. Adding highlight with 3727 and 3836.
13. Chunky French knots in C554.
14. Chunky twelve-strand French knots in 554.
15. Adding more French knots to edges in colours 33 and 327.
16. Blending with 3835 (I've embroidered only on the left-hand side to show the difference; continue to add the colour to the right-hand side also).
17. Add flashes of purple metallic.
18. Metallic stitches to sky.

Follow by adding the highlight to the top of each section in Light Antique Mauve colour 3727. You should just embroider to the line drawn on the template. At this stage, you will still have gaps in each section, apart from the two smallest sections on each side of the hoop.

Fill in the rest of each section in Violet colour 553, again only embroidering to the line. Notice how some of the large sections to the left blend Dark Lavender colour 209 with the highlighted colour 3727.

Working from the line down, starting with the lightest colours (Light Antique Mauve 3727 and Light Grape 3836), start embroidering the highlights, leaving the three main middle lower sections of the field.

Going back to colour 553, add little touches of shadow against colour 33. There are ten sections in total. Fading the darker colour into 209, French-knot thick lines to each section, the middle and lower section. The three main middle lower sections of the field need to have the largest number of French knots in colour 209. These should start as single French knots and gradually increase as you get to the edge of the hoop.

Fill in the rest of the middle section of the field in Medium Lavender colour 210. Following the lines you've created previously with Dark Lavender colour 209, French-knot in colour 210 on the lower part of the lavender bush. The very middle bush should create a triangle shape, ready to be filled with highlight.

Using the same colours to add highlight (colours 3727 and 3836), French-knot the last section of the bush.

Reworking the light sections and adding texture: These colours aren't in the colour chart, so it's more about free knotting where you feel the colours need blending, or where more texture is needed. There are no rules to these steps, and building up the knots is a matter of personal preference.

In Light Purple colour C554, double the floss and French-knot in each highlight section, keeping to the very bottom of the field. As you embroider back along the bushes, decrease the number of strands of floss to the original six and continue to French-knot over the highlights. Also scatter French knots in colour 210, and a small amount in colour 209.

Adding more texture to the centre of the three front bushes, in Light Violet colour 554, double the floss, creating twelve strands, and randomly add French knots over the highlighted centre.

Start to darken the edges of the bushes (where the purple meets the greenery) with colour 33, scattering the French knots from the original line of 33, and fading them along into the lighter colours. Again, do this only on the three main bushes. With colour 327, split the floss into three strands and add dark tones to that line, moving into the lighter tones here and there.

This is the last purple shade used to blend the harsh line made with colour 33. Scatter French knots along this line with Medium Grape colour 3835—this could blend colours 33 and 553 together.

The last stage is to add flashes of metallic thread to the darker areas of the field, in colour E3837. French-knotting to the right-hand side, scatter them wherever you feel it needs the light effect. These are created with all strands of the floss.

An extra step you can do is add a flash of light in the blue sky with a metallic silver thread, E415. Split the floss into a single strand and stitch over the whole sky, at random, with a long stitch.

MOUNTAINSCAPE WITH FLORAL FIELD

Thread painting is a relatively new term. It means using embroidery stitches to create a look that resembles paint strokes. There are various embroidery techniques that can be considered thread painting, for example, using only one strand of thread to embroider a mix of long and short stitches. Or you can use more strands to embroider chunky stitches and create the effect of broader strokes of paint in an Expressionist painting style. If your embroidery looks like a painted piece of art at the end, then it's a thread painting. I've come up with a pattern that allows you to create an Expressionist sky, where sections of colour resemble chunky brush strokes. The colours aren't blended together but still look like a faded sky, and textures can be added in. There are a lot of colours in this thread painting; some you will only need a few stitches of. Keeping that in mind, my patterns don't have to be followed exactly—changing the colour palette is encouraged.

What You Need:

- Five-inch embroidery hoop
- DMC thread: colours for the sky 02, 06, 168, 437, 543, 676, 712, 738, 775, 842, 945, 948, 977, 3771, 3865

- Cotton or linen fabric
- DMC thread: colours for mountain 336, 413, 414, 451, 452, 648, 739, 931, 934, 935, 3371, 3799, 3861, 3863

1.　**Template on page 171.**

2.　**Tranferred to fabric.**

Sky

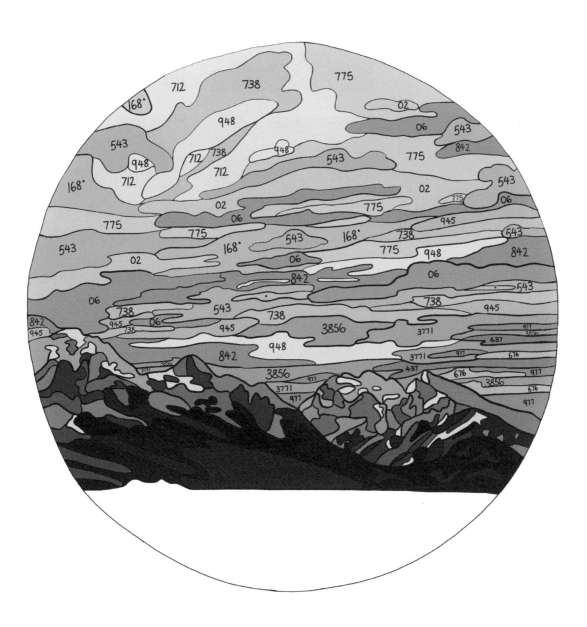

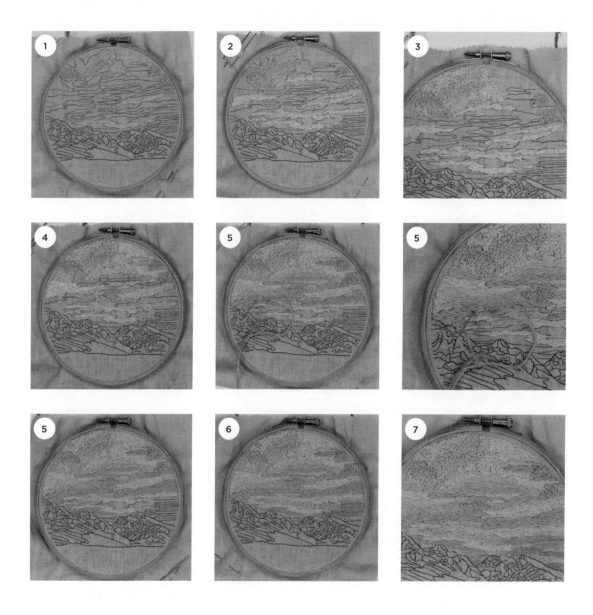

1.   Working with 543 and 943.

2.   Horizontal long-and-short-stitched
     sections, adding in 738.

3.   Adding 712. Mix of tight and loose
     French knots.

4.   Blue shades.

5.   Chunky sections with six strands.

6.   Blending with three strands.

7.   Adding sunset with two strands.

Transfer the template to the fabric and place it in the embroidery hoop. Begin embroidering the clouds. I've embroidered with a mix of three strands and six strands of floss. Make some French knots neat and tight, and others loose. This increases the puffy look of the clouds and adds a beautiful texture. The more French knots you add, the more three-dimensional they turn out. Why not keep building them up for a crazy amount of beautiful texture? The clouds are in four sections, going from Very Light Peach colour 948 in the middle, to the darker shade Ultra Very Light Beige Brown colour 543, framed with Very Light Tan colour 738, and finished with the lightest shade, Cream colour 712.

The sky can be a little overwhelming at the start—just keep referring back to the colour chart provided. It acts as a paint-by-numbers key. Each colour section should be stitched horizontally, using long and short stitches, with a small amount of satin stitching in the tiny sections. With the four colours used for the clouds, continue using them throughout the sky. These colours are stitched using three strands of floss.

Following on with the blue shades—Very Light Baby Blue colour 775, Very Light Pewter colour 168, and Grey colour 02—these are stitched using only two strands of floss.

The next sections of colours—Medium Light Driftwood colour 06 and Very Light Beige Brown colour 842—are stitched with six strands of floss.

Blending the sky together with Tawny colour 945, Ultra Very Light Mahogany colour 3856, and Light Tan colour 437, using three strands of floss.

Finishing the sky off with a sunset in Medium Light Terracotta colour 3771, Light Golden Brown colour 977, and Light Old Gold colour 676. These sections are stitched in two strands of floss.

Mountains

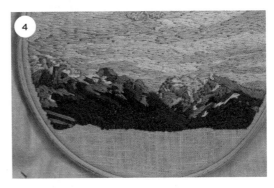

1. Using 935, 934.
2. 931, 414, 336, 3371, 3863.
3. 451, 3861, 3799.
4. Adding light tones, 648, 739, 452.

For the mountain section, you will use six strands of embroidery floss. The direction of the stitches isn't written in stone; you can be freer here, choosing which way you want them to lie. You just need to think about the bigger sections. Make sure you choose a direction that allows you to create long stitches. The larger green section at the front of the mountain is created with Dark Avocado Green colour 935, with a collection of French knots. Continue with the same colour and fill in the sections above with long stitches. Repeat with Black Avocado Green colour 934.

Follow on with the rest of the colours in the mountain; keep referring back to the colour chart to see where small details of colour are needed. Don't worry if a couple of colours are stitched in the wrong place; the shades are quite similar and, if the light tones are in the correct place, everything will still balance out.

Flower Field

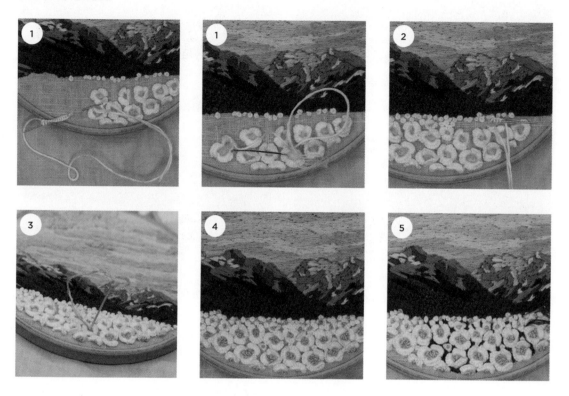

1. Three cast-on stitches to create a flower.
2. French knot where mountain meets.
3. French knot middle of flowers.
4. Add a few French knots to the where the mountains start.
5. Adding greenery.

As you can see, I haven't created a pattern to follow for this section. It's been left for interpretation. If you don't feel confident in your cast-on stitch, there are others you can use that would just be as successful. Go to page 178 for the Wildflower pattern template—you can trace the three-petal flowers from that pattern and fill in with satin stitch.

The flowers are made up of three cast-on-stitched petals. You want them to be close together, with the sides of the cast-on stitches touching each other. These are stitched with colour Blanc, using all six strands of floss. In the empty space, the flowers need to be in the middle of this section.

Keep in mind that the closer you get to the mountains, the smaller the flower would look, so the most effective way of showing this would be with tiny French knots. French-knot all along this line, where the mountains meet, in colour Blanc. Don't worry about the tiny gaps; these will be filled later.

Inside all the cast-on flowers, fill with French knots in Light Old Gold colour 676. Using the same green used in the mountains, Dark Avocado Green colour 935, embroider small vertical straight stitches in the gaps between the flowers.

CHAPTER 4:

HAIR EMBROIDERY

GIRL WITH RIBBON

I remember going on holiday in the '90s as a child and being fascinated with postcards. I was especially drawn to the ones with embellishments: ruffled lace added to the photographs to create Spanish skirts, tiny beads added to necklaces, and these sweet painted girls with threaded hair and woven hats. Naturally, I collected them throughout the years—which brings me to the present day, and my desire to push the boundaries of what has to stay inside the embroidery hoop. I've created this embroidery of a girl looking away, showcasing her brown ponytail and an unusual embroidery technique that I'm going to share with you.

What You Need:

- Fabric that doesn't stretch, like cotton, cotton linen, or calico
- DMC embroidery floss: Blanc, 152, 224, 225, 680, 727, 780, 819, 842, 3347, 3779, 3845
- Tapestry and milliners needles
- Seven-inch embroidery hoop

Prepping

For this project, you can use any skin-coloured cotton that holds its shape when in the hoop and is plain enough that you will be able to see the template to trace on the design. When choosing the fabric, of course, consider what colour skin you want the girl to have, because the fabric for the side of the face, back, and hand will be free of embroidery. When it comes to transferring the design, all the marks need to be covered with thread. I find it best to use a heat transfer pen for the skin and hair.

Tip: If you don't have a light box, you can tape the template onto a window and place the fabric over the template to trace on the pattern.

Jeans

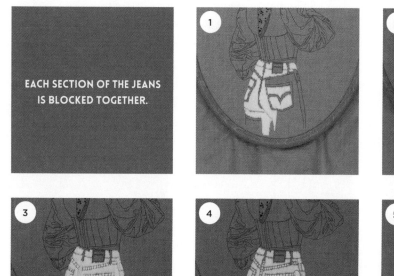

EACH SECTION OF THE JEANS IS BLOCKED TOGETHER.

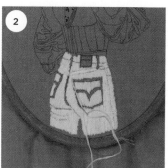

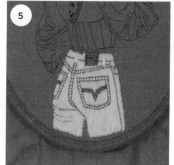

1.   Sections of satin stitch.
2.   Long stitches framing detail.
3.   Adding tacks inside with single strand.
4.   Couch stitch.
5.   Satin-stitch the patch and pocket detail.

Begin by filling in the jeans with long satin stitches in one colour. Starting with colour Blanc, you'll need to split the floss into three strands so there's more control with the satin stitch. Normally I wouldn't suggest having your stitches this long—especially when using satin stitch, because it tends to lift—but this embroidery is intended to stay in the hoop, so the fabric and stitches will stay taut. In this case, the hoop is needed to maintain the effect. Each section of the jeans is blocked together; some go in a slightly different direction to keep the shape of the jeans. I've marked which direction to stitch in the diagram. For example, the stitches to create the belt loop should be longer than the waistband is wide, and you'll use a small satin stitch section on the back leg to create a crease in the jeans.

To add the details to the jeans, use one strand of Dark Old Gold colour 680 with a mix of long and short stitches. Outline the pockets, yoke (the back area above the pockets), and side of the jeans with long stitches through the length of the area, and tack the stitches down with tiny stitches every so often (couch stitch). In the same colour, fill in the detail on the pocket with six strands of floss, and continue to the patch on the waistband. Outline the square first with the six strands and tack down with a single strand, then fill in with a satin stitch of six strands. Lastly, add the long belt loops with Blanc, using six strands of floss. These stitches need to be chunky, so keep adding to achieve the desired shape.

Outlining

Back-stitch along the outline, weaving each stitch.

You will leave the skin area empty of embroidery to allow the colour of the fabric to show. This technique has become a trademark element for my hair embroidery projects. To outline the face and hand, split the floss into two strands. Using Very Light Beige Brown colour 842, use a whipped back stitch over each line. Start by embroidering with a back stitch and weave in each stitch with two strands to create whipped back stitch.

Blouse

The blouse is made up of five shades of pink. The idea is to block these colours in, changing the direction of the stitches slightly so each section stands out. Each floss colour should be split into three strands. Start with the darkest shade, Medium Light Shade colour 152, then fill in the small sections to create shadow, followed by the lightest shade, Light Baby Pink colour 819.

The order the colours are embroidered in is 152, 819, 224, 3779, and 225.

Blend with the next shade, Vey Light Shell Pink colour 224, then Ultra Very Light Beige Brown colour 3779, and lastly Ultra Very Light Shell Pink colour 225. Please refer to the images on the next page, which shows the direction of each stitched section, to keep the shape of the blouse.

819

225

3779

224

152

1. **Darkest and lightest.**
2. **Adding 224.**
3. **Adding 3779.**
4. **Adding 225.**

Blue Option

Start with the darkest 825, then the lightest shade Ultra Very Light Blue colour 828, follow with Light Wedgewood colour 518, then Turquoise colour 597, and lastly Sky Blue colour 519.

Ribbon

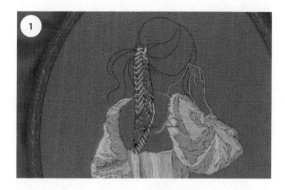 

1. Creating the stripes and adding French knots.
2. Satin stitch.

A mix of small stitches in different directions makes up the patterned scarf. Split each floss into three strands. With Medium Yellow Green colour 3347 and Very Light Topaz colour 727, stitch the stripes with small tack-like stitches, alternating the colours. Keep in mind that you don't have to strictly adhere to the pattern if you want to try something different. Follow the black dots with Very Light Terra Cotta colour 3779, stitching a French knot on each one. Fill in the rest of the scarf in Ecru with a satin stitch.

TO STITCH THE SCARF IN THE BLUE OPTION:

*   The stripes: Chilean Sunset colour 4130 and Light Tawny colour 951
*   French knots: Dark Blue, colour 825
*   Satin stitch: Light Tawny 951

Hair

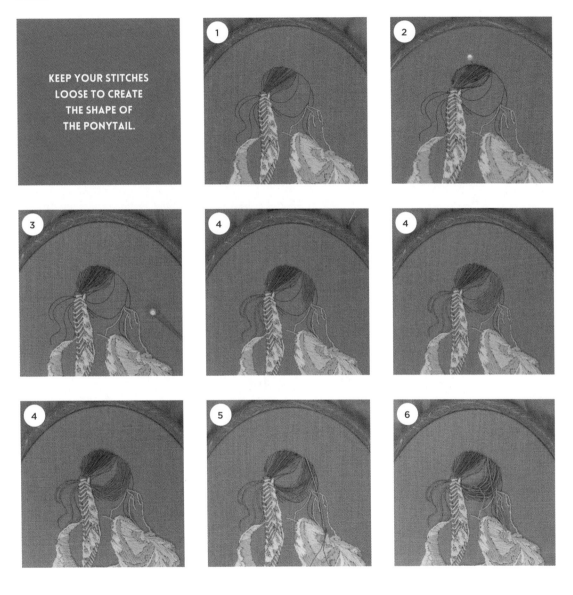

KEEP YOUR STITCHES LOOSE TO CREATE THE SHAPE OF THE PONYTAIL.

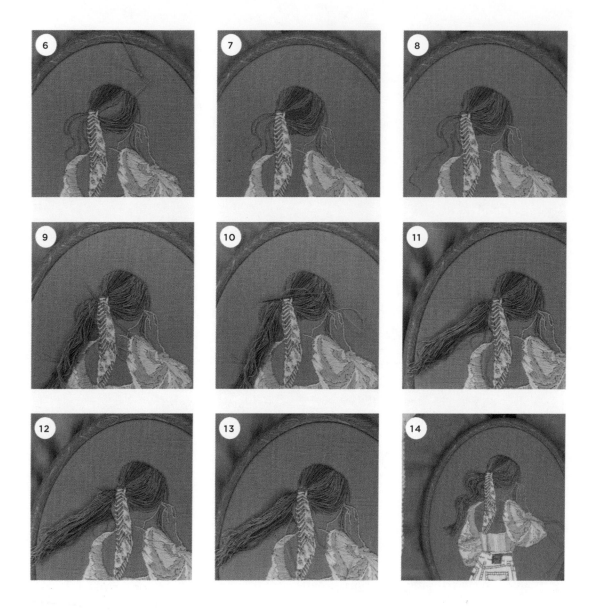

1. Long stitches.
2. Same section, layering with loose long stitches.
3. Using a pin to get the shape needed.
4. Direction of stitches for curved hair.
5. Curving thread with a weave.

6. Adding highlight.
7. Adding dark sections to hair.
8. Adding shape by weaving strands.
9. Weaving threads and knotting.
10. Creating a loop to knot.

11. Adding hair close to scarf into the front of the fabric and back through close to the original hole.

12. Go back through the fabric, making a loop, and bring the needle back through the front and in the loop.

13. Pull the loop tight and pull the thread off the needle. You will be left with two secure strands of floss on top of the fabric.

14. Tacking hair down close to the blouse.

Creating lifelike hair is a little unconventional. You need to keep your stitches loose to create the shape of the ponytail, and a lot of the hair will consist of simply anchoring the thread. For the hair, I've used colours 420, 680, 780, and 3845.

Cut a piece of floss to roughly arm's length and then split the floss into single strands. Start with the hair that will be tied back, both sides closest to the scarf. For this section use long stitches, almost like satin stitch. But for this project, the stitches don't have to be neat. Use Dark Hazelnut Brown colour 420 and Dark Old Gold colour 680. Once the section is full-looking, start to loosen your stitches as you add them to the fabric. Using the same colours, whipped-back-stitch the waves of the ponytail.

To create the hair that appears to be covering the girl's face, start by stitching straight sections to the top of the head. Change the directions of stitches when you hit the curve, and then again for the hair that hits the scarf, again using colours 420 and 680. Once the section is full, shape needs to be added. Starting at the top of the head, weave the thread into a strand in the middle, and then back into the fabric at the end of the section (at the scarf). Repeat until you achieve desired shape. Add light tones with Dark Yellow Beige colour 3845.

Follow along with the drawing, filling in each section of the head, making sure the middle hair section is the darkest colour. To do this stitch with Ultra Very Dark Topaz colour 780, use the same technique as before, filling with short stitches. I've also added a dark thread under the very bottom of the hair. Once filled, add shape by weaving the thread through those stitches with colours 420 and 680.

Don't forget to embroider the chunk of hair the girl is holding in her hand—this is a mixture of the two main colours, 420 and 680, with the light colour 3845.

Creating the ponytail is my favorite part. The whipped back stitch you created in the previous steps acts as a guide to the shape of the pony we are going to create. Start by cutting the strand of floss into a mixture of four- and six-inch sections. Next, stitch directly under the top line of the hair in the ponytail. Using all the colours to build the hair up, weave into the whipped back stitch, then create a loop to pull the thread though. This should create a tiny knot you can pull tight. Repeat this process, keeping the stitches very close together. Adding hair close to the top of the pony, where the scarf hangs, pierce the needle into the fabric from front to back and then back through to the front. Creating a tiny loop, come back through the front of the fabric, into that loop, and pull tight. Remove that strand of thread from the needle. Repeat this process, keeping the stitches very close together. Continue to add the strands into the fabric this way until you have achieved the look you would like for the ponytail.

To create the wavy shape, stitch small sections down. I've added a tiny stitch to the top wave and all along the edge of the blouse. Bend the "hair" to the shape you want and secure it. These tiny stitches are essential because, without them, the strands of threads aren't secured to the fabric, and you'll lose the wave shape of the ponytail.

Please note the last thing to do on this embroidery is to go back and embroider the brown detail on the jean patch. With colour 780, using all size strands, add two tack stitches.

GIRL HIDING BEHIND FLOWERS

This is a more advanced embroidery project given the number of colours used to create the flowing shirt. When you work on the shirt, be sure to follow the direction of the stitches I have indicated in the pattern, so the sections look cohesive. For the girl's hair, you will only need to use a straight stitch and a messy satin stitch. The styling of the hair can vary. I've chosen a long braid for this project, but you can leave it in a ponytail or twist it into a bun.

What You Need:

- Fabric that doesn't stretch, like cotton, cotton linen, or calico
- DMC embroidery floss: Blanc, Ecru, 152, 225, 367, 420, 422, 434, 437, 612, 613, 677, 746, 754, 818, 819, 3023, 3024, 3033, 3045, 3052, 3747, 3062, 3064, 3770, 3774, 3782, 3865, 3866, B5200
- Tapestry and milliners needles
- Seven-inch embroidery hoop

Prepping

For this design, I transferred the template to fabric using a printer. It's quite an intricate design, when it comes to the sections in the shirt and the very small details of the flowers. If this isn't a method you would like to do, tracing the template onto water-soluble fabric or straight onto fabric would be fine. You could even skip transferring the florals and add in your own. Using my printer creates permanent marks on the fabric. When it come to stitching, I will embroider just past the lines, so they don't show. In addition, I embroider the outlines thicker for the same reason.

1.   Template on page 174.

2.   Transferred to fabric.

Bag

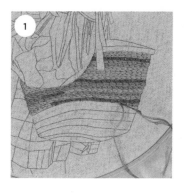

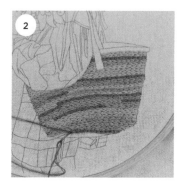

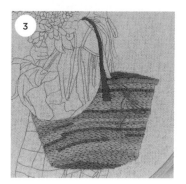

1.   Chain-stitching bag.

2.   Darker section on the bottom of bag.

3.   Satin-stitch opening of bag and straps.

To create the bag, use the colours Dark Hazelnut Brown 420, Light Hazelnut Brown 422, Light Tan 437, Light Drab Brown 612, and Yellow Beige 3045. Split the floss into three strands. Next, chain-stitch each section of the bag, using the colours at random. Don't worry about having your chain stitches fill whole sections; pick up where you left off with another shade. Also, the stitches don't need to be neat. The variety of stitches will cause the bag to appear woven. The last section on the bag needs to be the darkest shade, Dark Hazelnut Brown colour 420. Chain-stitch the bottom in this colour. Satin-stitch the opening of the bag with the same Dark Hazelnut Brown, keeping the stitches long.

To fill in the strap of the bag, use Light Brown colour 434. Begin by splitting the floss into two strands and satin-stitch horizontally up both individual straps.

Shirt Dress

The complex part of creating the shirt is using a large number of colours. There are twelve altogether. Embroidering these colours on the correct blocks and making sure the direction of your stitches is correct are the most important things in this step. The embroidery technique is a simple satin stitch. Again, it is completely fine if your satin stitch isn't perfect.

For the shirt, embroider in this order:

- Snow White B5200
- Blanc
- White 3865
- Ecru
- Ultra Very Light Mocha Brown 3866
- Very Light Brown Grey 3024

- Light Brown Grey 3023
- Light Mocha Brown 3782
- Very Light Drab Brown 613
- Very Light Mocha Brown 3033
- Very Light Tawny 3770
- Off White 746

Starting with the lightest colour, Snow White B5200, split the floss into three strands and satin-stitch each section of the shirt, keeping to the exact shape (six sections on arm, two sections and collar, two lower). Always refer back to the colour chart to keep you on track with the correct place to stitch.

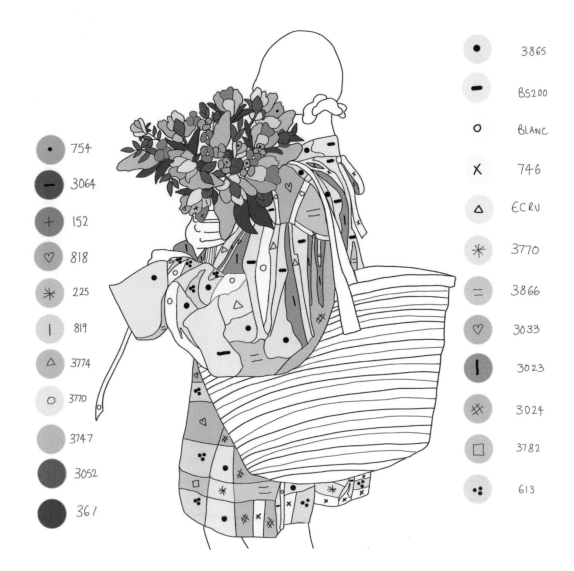

754
3064
152
818
225
819
3774
3770
3747
3052
367

3865
B5200
BLANC
746
ECRU
3770
3866
3033
3023
3024
3782
613

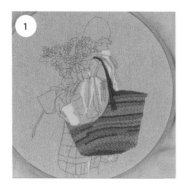

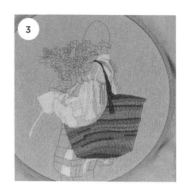

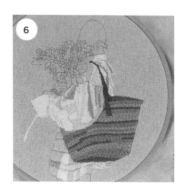

1.   Colour Blanc.
2.   Colour 3865.
3.   Colours Ecru, 3866.

4.   Colours 3023, 3024.
5.   Colours 613, 746.
6.   Colours 3033, 3770.

Colour Blanc: four sleeve sections, plus long cord hanging from cuff; two shoulder sections; one lower section under bag.

Followed by 3865: five sections on the sleeve, four small sections on the shoulder and collar, two sections on the skirt.

Ecru: seven small sections, all on the arm. In 3866, one section on the sleeve, one on the cuff, one on the shoulder, one on the back (near the top of the bag), and one on the button, under the bag.

Dark areas in 3023: ten sections from the cuff to the bow.

Light to dark areas 3024: one section on the arm, four sections on the skirt, under the bag.

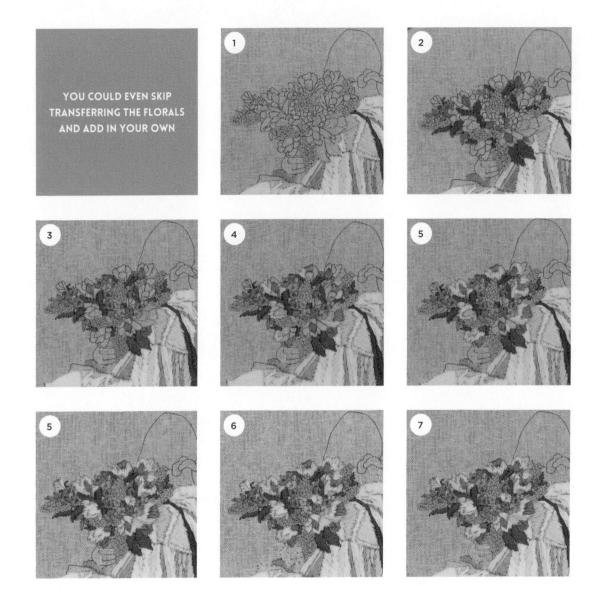

YOU COULD EVEN SKIP TRANSFERRING THE FLORALS AND ADD IN YOUR OWN

1. Violet flowers.
2. Greenery.
3. Granitos flowers.
4. Satin-stitch each section of the large flower.
5. Adding light sections
6. Back-stitch the outline.
7. Whipped back stitch.

Pull the colours together with 613, four sections on the sleeve and five sections on the skirt. Then add highlights with 746, four sections on the back and seven small sections on the skirt.

The last few colours: 3033 on the shoulder and two sections on the skirt, and two sections of 3770.

Flowers

If you have transferred the florals in the template, begin with the French knot sections. With Very Light Blue Violet colour 3747, split the floss into three strands and fill in the flowers marked in purple on the diagram, six sections in total. Once each section is filled in, I go back in and add more French knots in the centre, to create more depth.

To fill in the leaves, mix two shades of green: Medium Green Gray colour 3052 and the darker shade, Dark Pistachio Green colour 367. Split the floss into three strands and satin-stitch each leaf shape, with a couch stitch for the stem.

Continue using satin stitch, filling in the larger circle sections to give the look of a peony bud, in Desert Sand colour 3064, with three strands of floss. There are six sections in total.

This is the fiddly part, looking for the tiny three-petal flowers in the centre—these flowers are going to be built up with a series of granitos stitches. Stitch each petal until each section is full, using the same hole in the middle of the flower. These flowers are in Light Peach colour 754 and Medium Light Shell Pink colour 152, both with three strands of floss.

The rest of the larger and flatter flower shapes are achieved with three to four shades of pink, again with satin stitch. The petals in the front must be the lightest shade, fading to the next shade, with the darkest to the back. Stitch with the darkest to lightest shades; Medium Light Shell Pink 152, Baby Pink 818, Pink 225, Light Baby Pink 819, and Very Light Tawny 3770, referring back to the colour diagram. Repeat with the peach flowers and the rose buds, starting with Light Peach 754, Very Light Desert Sand 3774, Baby Pink 819, and Very Light Tawny 3770.

Once the flowers are complete, you'll notice a small empty section; this is to add the flower stems with the green shades 3062 and 367. Use a long stitch—the full length of the area—going from light to dark to fill up.

Embroider the skin with a whipped back stitch to outline. Try to match the colour of your fabric with your floss choice. Split the floss into three strands and back-stitch along the outline of the hand, neck, and legs. Using the same three strands, weave the floss in and out of the back stitch to create a whipped back stitch.

Hair

The hair is made up of four colours: the darkest colour, Dark Yellow Beige 3045, to the lightest shades, Off White colour 746, Sand Gold colour 677, and Ecru. Cut the floss to a length roughly twice the width of the embroidery hoop and split into single strands. Starting with the lightest colours, anchor the thread to the fabric and use long stitches to fill in the head (remembering to go past the outline of the head). Start out keeping your stitches tight; you'll notice that the bottom of the head becomes fuller, and there are still a lot of gaps to the top. Stitch from the top, but stop halfway down, evening out the density of the hair.

Once the fabric is covered, start to stitch a little looser, to give the illusion of hair and the shape of the head. To do this, all you need to do is to not pull the thread tight. All the stitches need to meet the scrunchy (ponytail band).

Once the head is completely covered, a sense of depth needs to be added to make the hair look more realistic. Using the darker shade Dark Yellow Beige colour 3045, start stitching from the scrunchy up to the head. These stitches are a quarter of the way up and should fan out.

THE STYLING OF THE HAIR CAN VARY. I'VE CHOSEN
A LONG BRAID FOR THIS PROJECT, BUT YOU CAN
LEAVE IT IN A PONYTAIL OR TWIST IT INTO A BUN.

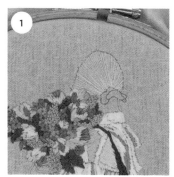

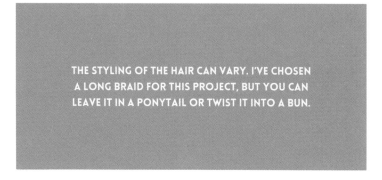

1. Stitching from the head to half the way down.
2. Stitching in the darker shade in a fan-like shape.
3. Adding single strands to the ponytail.
4. Going into the fabric from the front and back through to the front of the fabric.
5. Adding layers of strands underneath.
6. Ponytail thickness.
7. Braiding the ponytail.
8. Securing by wrapping one strand around the braid.
9. Cutting excess strands and tacking in place if needed.
10. Cast-on stitch.
11. Tack scrunchy in place.

To create the braid, cut eight-inch single strands in each of the four colours. For each strand of the ponytail, begin by stitching into the front of the fabric, adding a tiny stitch, and then coming back out the front of the fabric, and finally removing the thread from the needle. If you're going to braid the ponytail, then the tiny stitch isn't necessary. These stitches need to be very close together. Continue adding threads to the ponytail at the base of the head, where the scrunchy will be embroidered over. The thickness of the ponytail is a personal preference, so once you're happy with the number of strands in the ponytail, you can stop adding thread and move on to styling the hair.

I've braided the hair up to the bag, then secured it by wrapping one strand around the others and stitching it in place into the fabric. I've cut the length and waved the strands into place. If you would like to keep the shape, small stitches are needed.

To finish off this girl, cast-on-stitch the scrunchy, following the shape around. This is done in Blanc, six strands. Once you've stitched the scrunchy, you'll need to stitch it in place.

PORTRAIT

When I started creating the embroideries that showcase the quirky way I recreate realistic hair, the main reason I did it this way was that I didn't feel confident that I could embroider faces and be able to capture all their features. I also avoided filling in the skin tone and let my fabric become a focal point. This technique gave me the push to embroider a face, not worrying about it being anatomically correct or trying to manipulate embroidery techniques to achieve a certain look. I used the thread as if it were paint, adding in the highlights of the skin and filling in the shadow. Knowing when to stop was key—not overworking it, and letting the fabric become just as important as the embroidery. This embroidery focuses on the girl's accessories and key features of the face. The shadow and highlights aren't marked on the template. This allows you to be freer with your mark-making.

What You Need:

- Fabric that will provide the skin tone and doesn't stretch, like cotton, cotton linen, or calico
- DMC embroidery floss: Ecru, 19, 111, 315, 316, 420, 433, 434, 632, 680, 758, 779, 780, 801, 838, 869, 898, 950, 955, 964, 3726, 3771, 3781, 3802, 3861, 4145
- Anchor thread: 4501
- Tapestry and milliners needles
- Seven-inch embroidery hoop

Prepping

Before you start, it's best to plan out where the portrait will sit in the embroidery hoop. Place your fabric in the hoop and mark off where the hoop sits; this ensures that the template fits perfectly inside your chosen hoop size when it comes time to embroider. I have placed the template slightly off-centre and continued to transfer the template right up to the embroidery hoop. Keep

in mind that it will become difficult to stitch the edges to cover the marks you made. This design has been transferred to fabric using my home printer. It's one of the best methods for darker fabric.

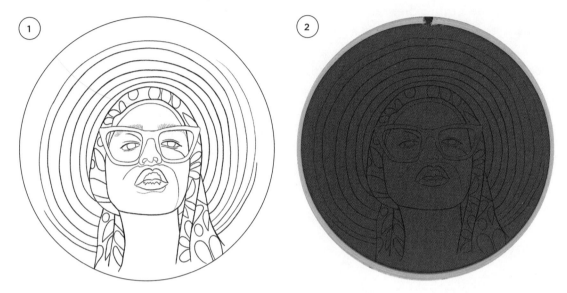

1.   Template on page 175.

2.   Girl transferred onto fabric.

Headscarf

To create the floral design, all you need is three different kinds of stitches: chain stitch, split stitch, and satin stitch. Starting with Ultra Very Light Terracotta colour 3771, split the floss into three strands and split-stitch the sections of the petals.

Next, use Very Light Terracotta colour 758, also split into three strands of floss. With this colour, chain-stitch the bigger petals. Satin-stitch the circles in Medium Light Autumn Gold colour 19, splitting the floss into three strands.

The leaf shapes are satin-stitched in Light Sea Green colour 964 and couch-stitched in Light Nile colour 955.

Fill in the rest of the scarf with a satin stitch in Light Desert Sand colour 950, curving the stitches around the head and using long vertical stitches on the two outer sections.

ALL YOU NEED IS THREE DIFFERENT KINDS OF STITCHES: CHAIN STITCH, SPLIT STITCH, AND SATIN STITCH.

1. Using chain stitch
2. Chain stitch and satin stitch.
3. Filling in the leaf shapes.
4. Using satin stitch to fill in the rest of the scarf.
5. Changing the direction of stitches for the last two outer pieces.

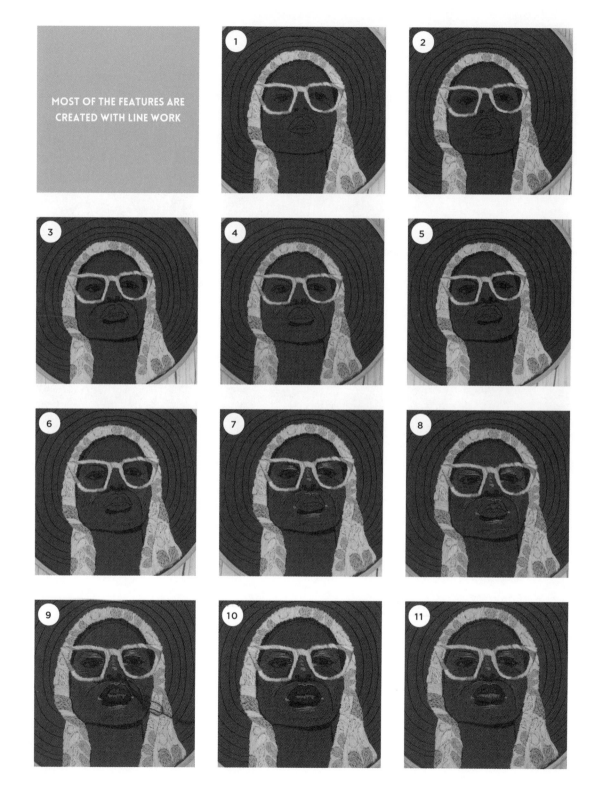

MOST OF THE FEATURES ARE
CREATED WITH LINE WORK

1. Start to fill in the shadow around the headscarf, the eyes, and lines around.

2. Adding the lighter shade to the forehead.

3. Adding the last of the shading.

4. Colour 632 with two strands of floss.

5. Using one strand of floss for the rest of the detail.

6. Blending the tones together with 779.

7. Adding contrasting highlight.

8. Adding colour to eyelids and lips.

9. Filling in the rest of the lip.

10. Blending top lip with colour 838.

11. Blending the bottom lip with a lighter shade, colour 316.

Filling in the Glasses

Filling in the glasses with variation thread.

To create the multicoloured glasses, I've used a variation thread which gives you all these colours in one. The beauty of this thread is that it turns out different every time. Using a satin stitch, go around the glasses vertically, but on a slight angle. This floss is Anchor colour 4501 and needs to be split into three strands for more control with the satin stitch.

Adding Facial Features

Most of the features are created with line work. To achieve this, you'll need to use stem stitch, long and short stitches, a whipped back stitch, and a satin stitch. With three strands of floss in Very Dark Beige Brown colour 838, outline the edge of the forehead with a satin stitch. Don't fill the whole section—only stitch the half of the space closest to the headscarf. Satin-stitch the middle of the eyes and fill in the detail with a stem stitch, in the same colour but only using one strand of floss. Also, satin-stitch the nostrils. Lastly, stem-stitch along the jaw.

To add lighter detail with Medium Brown colour 433, fill in the rest of the section around the forehead with three strands of floss, continuing around the eyelid. Split the floss into one strand and stem-stitch the detail under the eye, and the small shadow under the mouth.

Follow with Very Dark Coffee Brown colour 898. Splitting into three strands of floss, satin-stitch the rest of the shadow under the lips and stem-stitch the shade under the chin. Split the floss down to a single strand and fill in the shadow under the nose, using long and short stitches. Follow down the line using a stem stitch, with the same colour and a single strand. Outline the rest of the eye and the lower eye, and add small detail to the left-hand side eyelid. Continue to the right-hand side of the frames, adding a touch of colour with each stem stitch. Do the same on the other side of the glasses, but on the top left (closest to the eye).

Start to lighten with Ultra Very Dark Desert Sand colour 632, stitching long and short stitches to the cheek. Start with two strands of floss and then reduce down to a single strand as you get to the end of the cheek. Stay with the single strand of floss, continuing under the nose and lining one side of the lip. Add a touch of this colour to the chin, freely stitching a mix of long and short stitches together. Start to add colour near the eyes (through the lenses), to the very top of the nose (where the glasses meet) and the very top of the glasses, on the forehead. Finish off by adding long stitches to the left side of the forehead.

Blend the red tone with the brown fabric with Dark Cocoa colour 779, only using one strand of floss. Add long and short stitches to the cheek, until you get to the edge, on both sides. Add a small number of stitches to the chin, under the red colour. Finish off by following the shadow of the eye socket, with long single-strand stitches.

Now add a contrasting highlight with Light Cocoa colour 3861. Add long stitches horizontally across the eyelids, using a single strand of floss. Add small tack stitches to the corners of the eyes and down the highlight off the nose. Outline the top of the lip, the corner of the mouth, and the button of the lip, under the dark brown shadow.

Add colour to the eyes and lips using Antique Mauve colour 315, and, splitting the strands into two, add touches of purple to the rest of the eyelids. The stitches don't need to fill the area completely; small sections of the fabric can peek out. In the same colour, fill in the middle section of the top lip with a satin stitch. Go back to the glasses and fill in the rest of the bottom half of the lenses with Dark Mocha Brown colour 3781, using a satin stitch. Use a single strand of floss and keep the stitches long, the length of the area you are filling.

For the highlighted section on the bottom lip, satin-stitch with Dark Antique Mauve colour 3726. Fill in the rest of the lip in Very Dark Antique Mauve colour 3802, using a satin stitch to keep to the shape of the bottom lip, and again with the top.

To blend the lip colours together, blend with a single strand of Very Dark Beige Brown colour 838, adding long stitches to the top lip. Make sure you keep the shape of the stitches, and shorten the stitches as you reach the edge of the lip.

Add highlight to the bottom lip in Medium Antique Mauve colour 316, using a single strand of floss and keeping to the shape of the stitches already there.

Creating the Woven Hat

The woven hat is so large that it serves as a background for this piece. Using a basket-weave stitch, this will become the centre of the artwork. To achieve the woven hat look, you will need a mix of nine colours, used at random. With colours Ecru, 111, 420, 433, 434, 680, 780, 869, and 4145, split the floss into three strands ready to weave. The first step of the weave is to add small stitches all around each curved section. These stitches should sit on the marked line and not necessarily line up with the next section. This step is stitched in colour 801, using two strands of floss.

Once the whole area is filled, you can start to weave the colours in and out of those stitches. When you reach the end of the hat, go into the fabric and start again, but come back through the fabric. Remember to weave alternately—for example, if you ended on an over-under, then your next layer will start on an over-under. Don't worry if your thread won't reach the end of the weave, just start a new one where the last thread was secured into the back of the fabric. This can also be with a different colour.

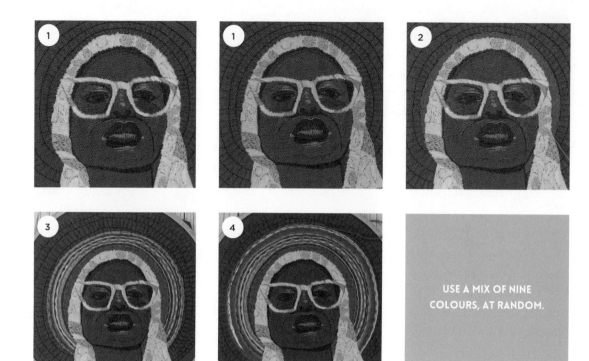

USE A MIX OF NINE
COLOURS, AT RANDOM.

1.   Setting up the weave stitch with small tacks.

2.   Start weaving with the section closest to the headscarf.

3.   Four sections woven.

4.   All the colours now used and repeated.

CHAPTER 5:

FLORALS

DRAWSTRING BAG

What You Need:

- Cotton fabric: I've used lightweight linen cotton
- Sewing machine or pinking shears: to overlock the fabric edges
- Thread suitable for the sewing machine or to hand-stitch the bag together
- DMC embroidery floss: Blanc, 318, 415, 524, 632, 950, 3022, 3064

- Milliners needle: long shaft, narrow eye for a smooth process
- Scissors
- Ribbon or cord
- Iron
- Stabiliser (optional)
- Safety pin

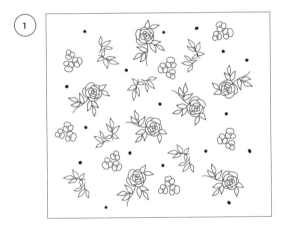

1. Template Page 176.

2. Transferred onto fabric

Embroidering the Bag

Hoop artwork.

If you're like me, you have a few projects going at once. Sometimes I add a few stitches to my current landscape, then set it aside and stitch a little rose to the latest doll I've been working on. I like to keep these projects separate, along with the supplies I need for them, because, as you can imagine, there are many thread colours I am actively using, along with the needles I use for each piece of work. Using project bags is a way to keep embroidery projects organised. They are perfect to pack up and use on the go, and are also a place to both store embroidery projects and keep the embroidery clean. They are easy to make and fun to decorate. Below is a step-by-step guide to making this single drawstring bag, along with a floral pattern that showcases three-dimensional stitches.

If you like this pattern, you can recreate it and keep it as a piece of hoop art, framed and hung on the wall. You could even embroider this pattern on a cushion or an item of clothing.

For this project, you'll need a 10-by-7-inch piece of fabric to embroider on. It's always easier to embroider on a larger surface of fabric, and then cut the fabric after. Place the fabric over the template to trace the design straight onto it, and put the fabric into an embroidery hoop. (I've used a heat transfer pen and a light box, but a window will work as well if you don't have a light box.) Keep the fabric taut—it helps keep control of the embroidery threads, especially when making complex stitches.

Filling in the Design

THREE-PETAL FLOWERS

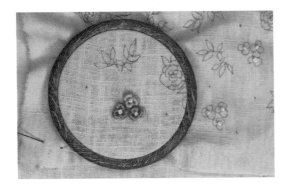

Bullion knot cluster.

Keeping the floss intact with all six strands in Very Light Golden Yellow colour 3078, embroider the centre of the each flower with a French knot. To create the petals, each section is a bullion knot. Two of the flowers are in Light Steel Grey colour 318, and one flower in Pearl Grey colour 415. When building up your bullion knot, wrap the thread around the needle roughly fifteen times. The more thread you wrap onto the needle, the more three-dimensional and curved the stitch will be. If the bullion knot is too raised for your liking, a simple anchor stitch can be added to secure it to the fabric.

LEAF

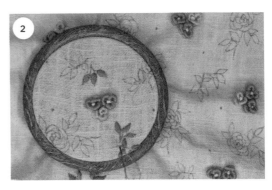

1. Satin-stitch leaf.

2. Couch-stitch, securing the stitch with one strand.

Use Trellis Green colour 522. The floss needs to be split into three strands, so the stitches are more controlled and lie flat to the fabric. Using a satin stitch, fill in each leaf shape. Remember to keep the threads tight and stitch on the line; this will help to keep the shape of the leaf. For the stem, couch-stitch with one strand. The leaves on roses are in Light Fern Green colour 523. Use the same technique on the previous page.

ROSES

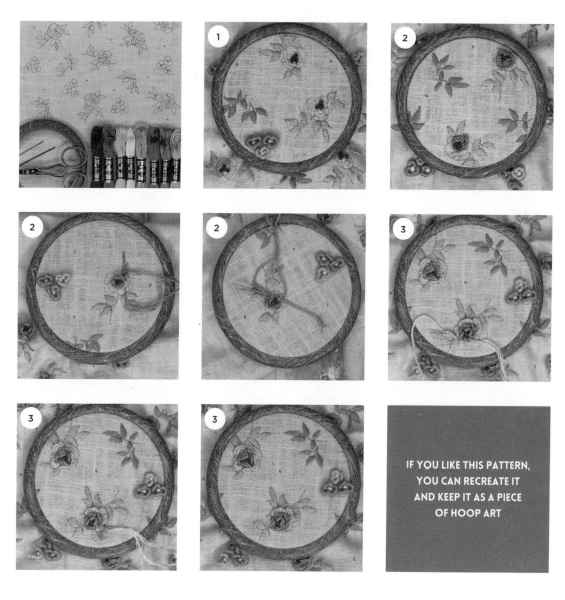

IF YOU LIKE THIS PATTERN, YOU CAN RECREATE IT AND KEEP IT AS A PIECE OF HOOP ART

1.   French knot centre with three around.
2.   Building up rose with cast-on stitch with colour 3064.
3.   The outside of the rose in colour 950.

To create the roses, you need to use all six strands of floss in Ultra Very Dark Desert Sand colour 632. Stitch a French knot in the centre of each rose; for the shapes surrounding the centre, satin-stitch these three sections using the same colour. This section can be hidden when the rose layers are added; it helps to create depth. Following the shapes I've created, start to build up the rose. The number of knots you add to your needle will depend on the size of the shape you are filling. This guide acts as a mark to where the cast-on stitch starts and ends (see page 19 for a diagram of cast-on stitch technique). You'll need to use all six strands in Desert Sand colour 3064. Embroider four to five sections of the rose with a cast-on stitch. As each cast-on stitch is built around, you will start to see your rose take shape. Again, keeping the floss intact and using all six strands, in Light Desert Sand colour 950, add the outer section of the rose. These cast-on stitches should cover the previous colour.

DOTS

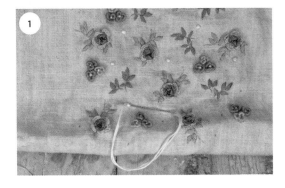

1.   Chunky French knot.

2.   Finished pattern.

Embroider a French knot over each dot in colour Blanc. I've doubled the thread (so twelve strands total) to create a full, thick French knot.

Embroidery Options

If a cast-on stitch or bullion knot is a little too difficult for you, or you would prefer your embroidery to be flat to the fabric, then using a satin stitch would work just as well. Fill in each separate section, keeping the shape of the rose that is drawn.

OPTION TO ADD INITIAL

Personalising your creation is always a nice touch. If you want to add an initial, I would do so when you first draw the design onto fabric. This way you have more control over the final design and continuing the pattern around it.

Tip: Pulling the threads too tight will cause the fabric to pull or bunch, so be sure to keep the fabric taut in the hoop. This will help your stitches stay tight and will be less likely to slacken when the fabric is taken out of the embroidery hoop. The idea is to create a "satin" look. The satin stitch does take some practice, though, so don't be discouraged if your first attempt doesn't come out perfect. Your technique will improve with practice!

Finishing Your Stitches

When you begin to run out of thread, be sure to secure your work by knotting the remaining thread a few times on the back side of your project. A stabiliser can be ironed on the back for extra security, depending on what fabric you've used. Remember: this could change the nature of your fabric if the fabric is delicate.

Construction

The Drawstring Bag

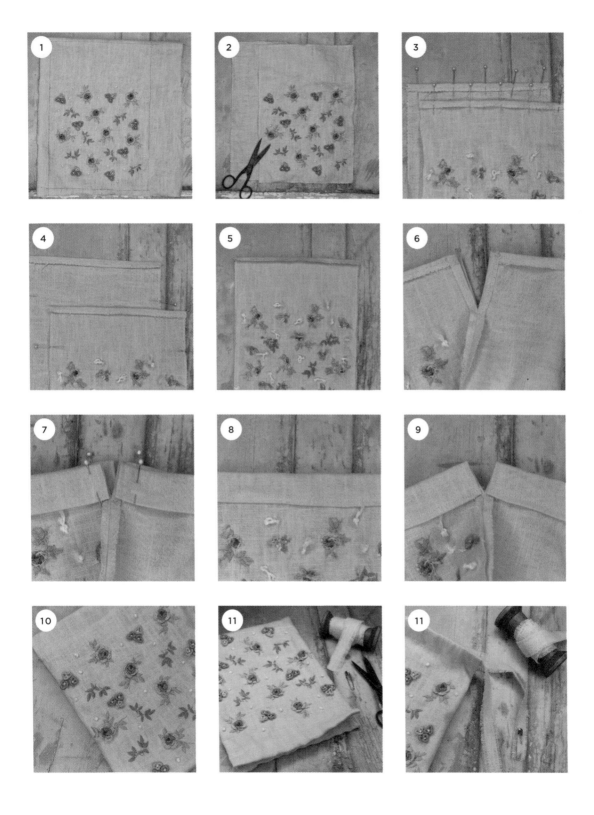

PERSONALISING YOUR
CREATION IS ALWAYS A
NICE TOUCH.

1.   Drawn 10-by-7 box to cut.
2.   All four sides overlocked.
3.   Quarter-inch fold pressed flat.
4.   Pin acts as a marker for where you start
     and finish sewing.
5.   Stitch the bag together.
6.   V-shaped stitch.
7.   Line seam to the bottom of the V.
8.   Stitch all the way around.
9.   View from the drawstring opening.
10. Turn the bag right-side-out.
11. Threading drawstrings with safety pin.
12. Drawstrings thread through.
13. Edges sewn together.

Once you have embroidered the floral design, cut two pieces of fabric into a 10-by-7-inch rectangle and prevent all edges from fraying with the overlock stitch on the sewing machine (you can also use pinking shears, which will work just as well).

On the reverse side of the fabric (the back of the embroidery), fold over a quarter-inch on the top of each piece of fabric to create a clean, crisp edge. Then iron flat to keep the edge.

Put the two pieces of fabric together. Measure out two inches on each side from the quarter-inch fold and place a pin there for reference, to indicate the beginning point of where you want to stitch.

Sew around the other three sides, again a quarter-inch from the edge.

Note that you want to stitch them together so the two "right" sides of the fabric are facing each other. This means when we turn the bag inside out, the "right" way, all the seams are inside. Again, if you don't have a sewing machine, a simple tacking stitch or back stitch would work fine.

Next, open out the seams and press flat. You'll also press the two-inch seam allowance that is marked with pins. After your seams are flat, stitch around the opening from the top of the fabric, down to the pin and across to the other side of the fabric, joining the two pieces together (and up the other side). This makes something like a "V" shape.

To create the open seam for the drawstring to go in, fold over the top of the bag; the edge of the fabric should meet the bottom of the V shape just stitched. Pin in place and stitch down to secure.

Turn the bag right-side-out.

To add the drawstring, you'll need roughly a yard of ribbon or cord. I've used the same fabric as for the bag. Insert the string into one side of the seam, and pull it through and out on the other end of the seam. Repeat the process on the other side of the bag. Once you have both ends of the drawstring threaded through the openings, knot them together.

PINCUSHION

I'm terrible at keeping track of my needles, often having to replace them. It's always handy to have a place for them on your workspace; why not create one that's just as beautiful as it is handy? This project is fun and easy. It requires only five kinds of stitches, and produces an embroidery that creates delicate three-dimensional flowers that stand off the fabric once the pincushion is stuffed. Like all my projects, you don't have to turn the final embroidery into a pincushion; you could also keep it as a piece of art.

What You Need:

- Stretchy fabric: I've used a velvet Lycra
- Tapestry needle: size 16, thick shaft
- Four-inch embroidery hoop: I've used a flexible hoop with a wood effect

- DMC embroidery floss: Blanc, 224, 316, 340, 341, 371, 422, 524, 597, 754, 964, 3064, 3354, 3363, 3726, 3774
- Scissors, glue, card stock, toy stuffing

Getting Started

Begin by tracing the template onto the fabric. I've used DMC Magic Paper—a water-soluble fabric—for this project because the project will need to be embroidered onto stretch fabric to create the stuffed dome pincushion shape. This can distort the template if it's transferred directly. It works best if you choose something stretchable, such as velvet Lycra.

You'll need a lot of fabric around this design, so cut a six-inch square and pop it into an embroidery hoop. Keep the fabric taut and don't worry about the placement—we will be repositioning the finished embroidery at the end.

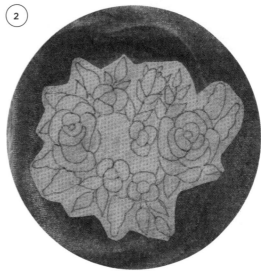

1.   **Template on page 177.**

2.   **Transferred onto fabric**

Filling in the Design

PEACH ROSE

Begin with six strands of floss in Desert Sand colour 3064, which is the darkest shade of the rose. French-knot the centre, followed by two cast-on stitches around the French knot.

Repeat the cast-on stitch for Light Peach colour 754, again, placing the stitches around the last colour, building up the rose. You should have five sections in total. With the last cast-on stitch, I have made the petal longer by using two needles when I twist the floss onto it. To do this, insert the second needle into the fabric before you twist the floss onto the needle. When you twist the floss, go around both needles. Once you have the desired amount on, pull out the second needle, as it's not needed anymore, and continue to pull the floss off the attached needle to sit on the fabric. You'll notice there are gaps where the cast-on stitches meet. To fill in this space, secure the cast-on stitches with a tiny stitch, making sure you stitch under the previous cast-on stitch (see picture 5, pincushion, for help). You should continue so that the fabric is completely covered. See [Insert image 5pincushion] for where I tack the stitches.

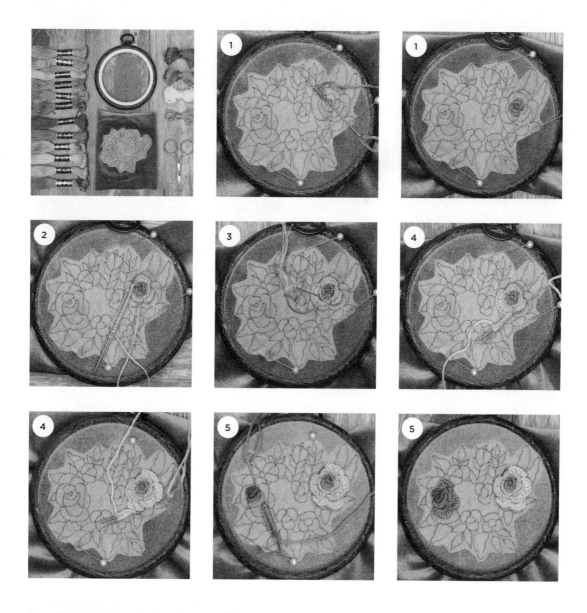

1. French knot centre with two cast-on stitches around it.
2. Building up rose in colour 754. Using two needles to create bigger petals.
3. Securing the cast-on stitches in place.
4. Using two needles to create bigger petals.
5. Darker rose.

To create the final part of the flower, add the rest of the cast-on stitches around the right-hand side of the rose, in Very Light Desert Sand colour 3774. There should be five stitches in total. Again, these petals are larger than the centre of the rose, and I have used two needles to create a bigger cast-on stitch (see page 19 for a diagram of a cast-on stitch).

Repeat the same technique for the other rose, starting with the darkest shade, Dark Antique Mauve colour 3726, then Medium Antique Mauve colour 316, and finally Very Light Shell Pink colour 224. Use the same technique with two needles as you get to the outer petals of the rose.

THE ROSE BUD

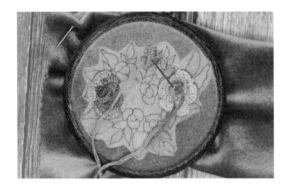

Layering the second cast-on stitch.

Stitching with six strands, begin by embroidering a French knot at the centre in Dark Antique Mauve colour 3726. Next, add the two lighter sections as cast-on stitches that will subtly layer over the French knot and create a bud effect. Employing the same technique as for the roses, in Light Dusty Rose colour 3354, add a cast-on stitch slightly over the previous stitch, so the bottom parts of the rose bud overlap. Add green finishing touches to the bud, in Mustard colour 371. Add three small stitches to the top of the bud and fill in the leaves below.

LEAVES

Stitching with six strands in colours Mustard 371, Very Light Fern 524, and Medium Pine Green 3363, fill in the leaf with a leaf stitch, slightly overlapping the bottom of each stitch. To create this effect, place a straight stitch at the point of the leaf, then continue to add stitches, each overlapping the previous stitch, until the leaf is covered.

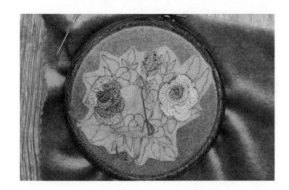

Leaf stitch.

Three-Petal Flowers

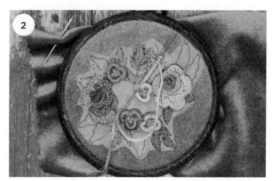

1. French-knot the centres.

2. Wrapped the needle 20–24 times.

Stitching with six strands, embroider a French knot to start the middle of each flower in Light Hazelnut Brown colour 422. To create the curved petals, stitch a bullion knot in Turquoise colour 597 and Light Sea Green colour 964. Again, this depends on the size of the shape that needs to be filled: the more thread you wrap around the needle, the more volume you add to the petal, and it will obviously stand up more from the fabric.

There really are no rules; it will just make your flowers more or less three-dimensional. I've wrapped the needle twenty to twenty-four times to create this volume (see page 17 for a diagram of a bullion knot).

ELDERFLOWER

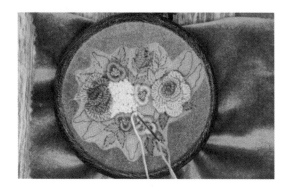

Layering the French knots.

To create the elderflower, French-knot the whole section with six strands in colour Blanc, filling the empty space and joining the flowers together. You can layer the French knots up to create height.

LAVENDER

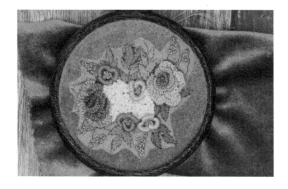

Mixing shades for lavender.

Stitching with six strands in Medium Blue Violet colour 340 and Light Blue Violet colour 341, embroider a series of French knots to cover the entire section, mixing the two colours. You should have five lavender branches in total.

THE STEMS

A couch stitch creates the stems; split the floss into two strands and stitch the stem of each leaf branch and the flower stems. Secure the stitch down with one strand, using the corresponding colour 371, 524, or 3363, to match the leaves.

Once you have completed the embroidery, wash away the water-soluble fabric or Magic Paper. Take the embroidery out of the hoop and run it under warm water, and the soluble fabric will dissolve. Instead of submerging it, you can also spray it with a water bottle. Let it dry.

1.   Tacking couch-stitch down.

2.   Wash away the Magic Paper.

Creating the Pincushion Shape

To create the stuffed pincushion shape, set the embroidery back into the hoop. Begin by pulling the fabric gently up and away from the hoop, to create room for the stuffing to fill it.

Next, using toy or cushion stuffing, roll a handful into a ball and pop it into the hoop until you like the shape. At this stage, you can go back in with French knots in colour Blanc and build up the density, creating more height and filling in the gaps.

Cut away the excess fabric, leaving roughly half an inch to glue down to the frame. Cut a four-inch circle out of card stock and a five-inch circle out of fabric. Do a running stitch around the edge of the fabric circle, place the card stock inside, and pull the thread tight. The fabric will cover the card stock perfectly. Don't forget to secure your thread.

Once you have added the stuffing, take the outer hoop off and sew the stuffing in with long stitches stretching across the diameter of the hoop. Glue the card stock insert onto the back. Cut another piece of fabric, roughly the shape of the hoop, and glue to the edges.

Pull the embroidery hoop back onto the pincushion from the back. Pop your pins and needles into the top, and voila! You have a darling pincushion. If you didn't want to make a pincushion and you'd like the embroidery to stay a piece of art, you can centre the florals and set it back into a hoop. I've used an oval wall-hanging mini embroidery hoop and turned the florals to the side; it frames it perfectly.

TO CREATE THE STUFFED
PINCUSHION SHAPE, SET
THE EMBROIDERY BACK
INTO THE HOOP

YOU DON'T HAVE TO TURN
THE FINAL EMBROIDERY
INTO A PINCUSHION; YOU
COULD ALSO KEEP IT AS A
PIECE OF ART.

1. Fabric pulled loose in the embroidery hoop.
2. Adding more white French knots.
3. Running stitch around outside of circle.
4. Place card stock inside and pull fabric tight.
5. Glue the edges of the card stock and insert to the back of the hoop.
6. Stuffing pushed into the back of the hoop.
7. Gluing backing on.
8. Gluing another circle shape to hide glued edges.
9. Keeping embroidery as a wall hanging.
10. Oval hoop.
11. Finished pincushion

DENIM JACKET

I've created floral templates that allow you to design your own jacket. Or you can mix and match patterns to create your own. You can transfer small sections of each template and keep adding flowers to the stem, or repeat the pattern continuing down the back of your jacket. The possibilities are endless. To achieve the vibrant floral jacket project here, I use four stitching techniques: satin stitch, couch stitch, French knots, and bullion knots.

What You Need:

- Jacket
- DMC thread: Blanc, Ecru, 165, 367, 725, 726, 727, 729, 758, 782, 834, 951, 987, 3348, 3820, 4128, 4508
- DMC Magic Paper
- Chenille needle and milliners needle

All four templates found on pages 181-182.

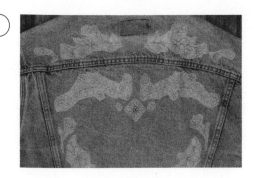

1.   Template transferred on Magic Paper and placed on back of jacket.

2.   Floral patterns 1, 2, and 3 used.

To begin, transfer the template to your jacket. I've used DMC Magic Paper to trace the template onto the fabric. Feel free to play around with the design. You can add as many or as few of the floral designs to your jacket as you like.

Floral 1

Most of these stitches are simple, for clean lines and blocked colour. For this project, you don't need to use an embroidery hoop. Embroidering without a hoop helps you control the tension of the satin stitch so the stitches don't sag, and you'll know how they will lie on the jacket.

Using a satin stitch, with six strands of floss, fill in the leaves, using Light Yellow Green colour 3348. Stitch each section on a slight diagonal to keep the shape of the leaves. French-knot the centres of the two larger flowers, again with six strands of floss, in Medium Light Topaz colour 725. Satin-stitch the middle of the outer flower in the same colour. Satin-stitch the petals of the closed flower in Very Light Topaz colour 727. Next, fill in the petals with Blanc, using all six strands of floss. I stitch from the middle of the petal and work my way around it to keep the shape of each curved petal. Finish off the flower by couch-stitching along the stem, joining the leaves and flowers together. This is with Very Light Golden Olive colour 834, using all six strands of floss, then securing down (adding the tacks to the long stitch) with one strand.

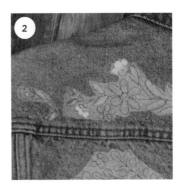

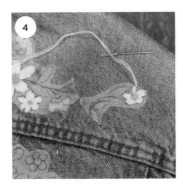
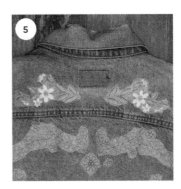

MOST OF THESE STITCHES ARE SIMPLE, FOR CLEAN LINES AND BLOCKED COLOUR

1. Satin-stitch each leaf.
2. Stitching the middles of the flowers.
3. Filling in the petals in Blanc.
4. Stitch the middle of each petal first, building up the shape.
5. Couch-stitch the stem.

Floral 2

Using the same technique as on the previous page, in Dark Pistachio Green colour 367, couch-stitch along the stem using six strands of floss, and then tack the stitches down with one strand.

Next, using Ecru, satin-stitch the leaves on the flower beside and in the middle of the mirrored flower. On that same flower, satin-stitch each petal separately, so each is distinct. Do the same for the two small flowers.

The mirrored flower is created with the inner petals found on the Floral 1 template. It is repeated four times, each joined at the centre.

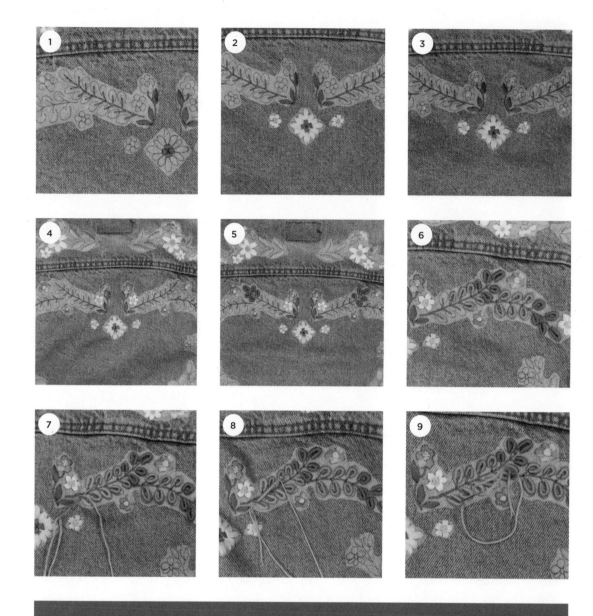

STITCH FROM THE MIDDLE OF THE PETAL AND WORK AROUND
IT TO KEEP THE SHAPE.

1. Adding dark green.
2. Satin-stitch the petals.
3. Stitch the centres of the flowers.
4. Filling in the flowers with an orange mix and white.
5. Bullion knots on the end of the branch in 782.
6. Follow on with a light shade for bullion knots.
7. Finishing off the branch with the lighter shade.
8. Wrapping the floss the length of the needle.
9. Pulling the thread off the needle and tight to the jacket. Tacking in place.

To begin, fill in the centre of each flower with a mix of French knots and satin stitches in Topaz colour 726, using all six strands of floss. Next, satin-stitch the petals with a variation of thread: Gold Coast colour 4128, and Winter White colour 3865. Now fill in the details on the branch using Dark Topaz colour 782. Begin by stitching a bullion knot on the end of the branch (you should have five on the inside branch and three on the other). You might want to secure the bullion knots to stay flush with the jacket.

Follow with a lighter shade, Medium Old Gold colour 729, stitching bullion knots on the next five to six buds. Finish off the last of the inside branch with a lighter shade again, Dark Straw colour 3820. You should now have three bullion-knotted buds.

Floral 3

For these flowers, begin with a French knot to the centres in Medium Light Topaz colour 725. Next, use a satin stitch to fill in the two smaller flowers. (These smaller flowers are found on the Floral 2 template.) The flower colours are Winter White colour 3865, for the smallest; Light Tawny colour 951, for the medium flower; and Very Light Terracotta colour 758, for the largest. For the bigger flowers, embroider the petals in two sections that join the satin stitch from the tip. Use the drawn line in the middle of the petal to guide where to stop and start the next satin stitch.

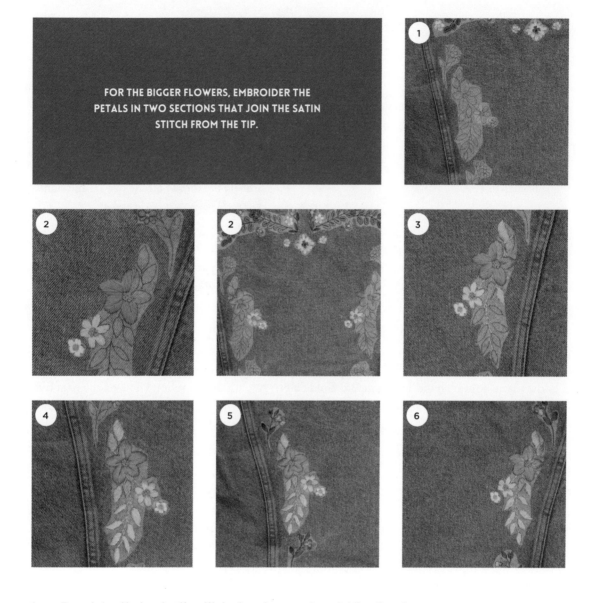

FOR THE BIGGER FLOWERS, EMBROIDER THE PETALS IN TWO SECTIONS THAT JOIN THE SATIN STITCH FROM THE TIP.

1. French-knotted and satin-stitched centres.
2. Satin-stitched large petals in two sections.
3. Adding green leaves.
4. Adding Ecru leaves.
5. Stitching the small flowers.
6. Adding yellow detail to the large flower.

Satin-stitch the leaves on a diagonal with a mix of two shades of green: Very Light Moss Green colour 165, and Very Light Golden Olive colour 834. Stitch both using six strands of floss. Add the stems with a couch stitch in colour 165, again using six strands of floss. Next, add long stitches and tack them in place with a single strand. Fill in the last seven leaves with Ecru. For the last flowers, use a satin stitch in a variation thread, Gold Coast colour 4128. For the leaves and stem, satin-stitch with Dark Forest Green colour 987. Add small touches of yellow to the large pink flower petals in Medium Light Topaz colour 725, with small tack-like stitches.

Font

(FOR MORE ON FONTS, SEE THE FONT CHAPTER ON PAGE 161)

If you would like to personalise your jacket—add your initials to the design, add text to the centre for an inspirational quote, or embroider a loved one's name and gift it to them—the following font works perfectly for all of these options. The letters can be joined together to create cursive writing or to make the words flow, which ties in perfectly with the floral embroidery.

Using water-soluble fabric, trace the font and pin it in place. Make sure you use a washable pen so when you rinse the solution away, the pen ink won't bleed into the fabric or embroidery thread.

To fill in the letters, use a satin stitch on a diagonal. As you get to the thinner sections, you need to embroider with a whipped back stitch. This will give you more control when the letters start to curve and loop. Split the floss into three strands for more control with the satin stitch. Use the same amounts of strands when stitching with a whipped back stitch as well.

For this project, I embroidered the words "she belongs among the wildflowers" with a variation thread, Frosted Countryside colour 4508. I spaced the words out to fit in the whole area of the back, leaving room to add another floral stem to the bottom. The daisy-chain effect I created is done with the Floral 1 template, using colours 727, 3348, 165, and Blanc, and using a satin stitch, French knots, and a couch stitch. The only thing left is to wash away the solution with warm water.

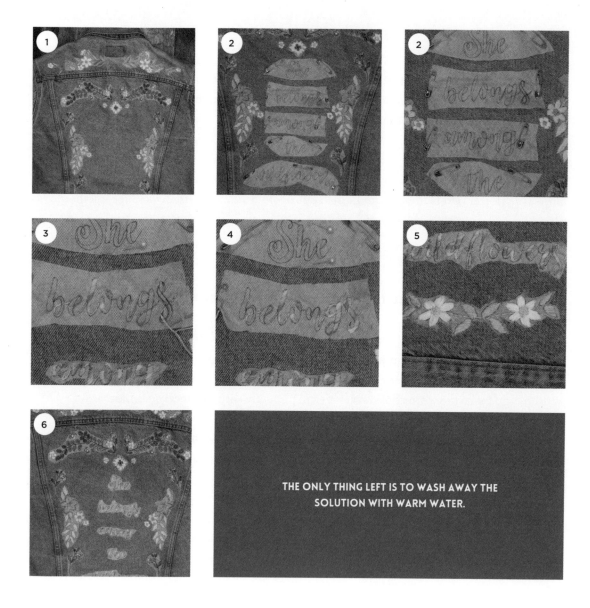

THE ONLY THING LEFT IS TO WASH AWAY THE
SOLUTION WITH WARM WATER.

1. Before personalization.
2. Tracing the font onto water-soluble fabric
   and pinning into place.
3. Using whipped back stitch to join the
   letters together and add the smaller detail
   to each letter.
4. Satin-stitching the larger sections of
   the letters.
5. Daisy chain on the bottom of the jacket.
6. With words added.

Most of the templates I have created can be manipulated and stitched onto a jacket; small sections can be taken from each option and arranged differently to become a unique and one-of-a-kind design. I have added tiny bees to my design—these can be found on the large (and the small) rose pattern.

CHAPTER 6:
INTERIORS AND EXTERIORS

MID-CENTURY LIVING ROOM

This project is a recreation of one of my first retro interiors. I've changed things around a bit and enhanced the texture since the original version. As with all of my templates, you don't need to follow every embroidery stitch I have used. If you prefer, you can fill the design with satin stitch or long and short stitches, which would still give an interesting result.

What You Need:

- Five-inch embroidery hoop
- Cotton or linen fabric
- DMC thread: 22, 355, 420, 434, 676, 680, 727, 732, 734, 743, 746, 801, 890, 918, 919, 922, 936, 975, 3347, 3371, 3776, 3777, 3782, 3820, Ecru, E436, E746

Template on page 183.

Transfer the template to fabric. If you don't want to stitch the whole of the hoop (i.e., the walls, ceiling, floor), you can choose a fabric that will make a nice background for this scene. You could even try a patterned fabric to give the look of wallpaper.

Wall

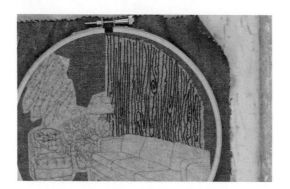

Outlining the wood panels and adding highlight.

To create the wood-grain panelled wall, divide the floss into single strands. In Black Brown colour 3371, stitch over every line, keeping the stitches long and securing in place with tiny stitches, like a couch stitch. Bend the stitches to fit the shape and then fix them in place to hold the shape. Once all the outlines are covered, use metallic Golden Oak light effect thread colour E436 with the same couch-stitch technique.

Plant

Satin-stitching section of leaves and pot.

Adding a houseplant was a must, so I decided on the very popular Monstera because the vivid green really pops with all the warm reds, oranges, and browns. The whole plant is satin-stitched using floss separated into two strands and stitched on a diagonal, keeping to the shape of the leaf and the tiny details. The three colours I used for the plant are Medium Yellow colour 3347, Ultra Dark Pistachio Green colour 890, and Very Dark Avocado Green colour 936. Fill in the pot on a diagonal in satin stitches with two strands of floss, in Medium Yellow colour 743. Add the small detail to the top and bottom of the pot in Light Old Gold colour 676. Also add colour to the leaf that covers the pot.

Chair

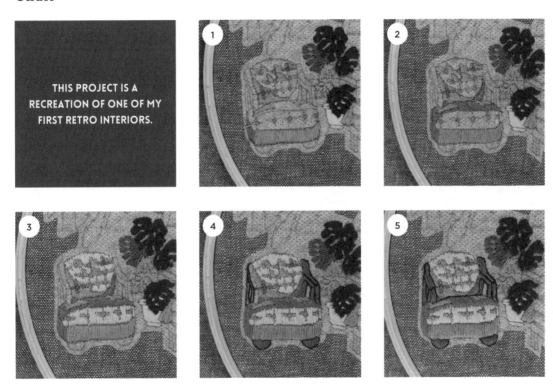

1. Adding detail with two sections of darker detail.
2. Filling in shading with satin stitch.
3. Filling in the chair with 676.
4. Outline the wood with single strand 3371.
5. Adding 434 to the wood on the armchair.

The armchair is created with slightly different directions of satin stitch in three shades of yellow, blocked in to create depth. Split the floss into two strands and start with Dark Old Gold colour 680. Stitch the tiny detail of the chair, and tack stitches with French knots in the centre of each circle, also filling in the shadows with a diagonal satin stitch. The details on the top right and bottom left of the chair need to be in a darker shade, Dark Hazelnut Brown colour 420, then continue the shading around it with colour 680, in satin stitch. Outline the wood arms with a single strand of Black Brown colour 3371, using a couch stitch. Fill in the area with Light Brown colour 434, splitting the strands into three.

Couch

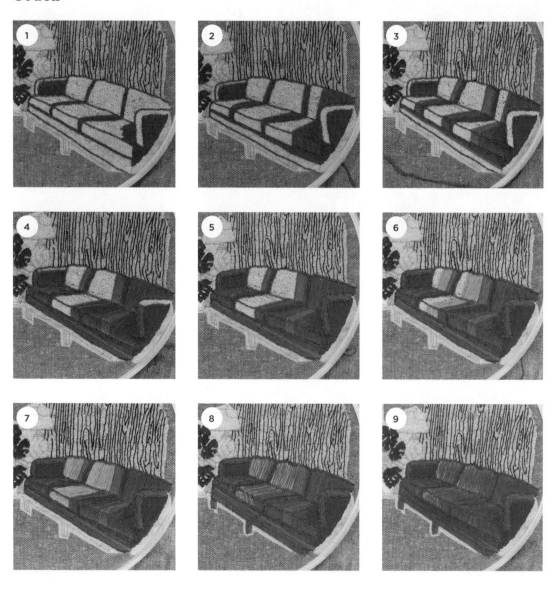

1. Outline the couch in 810, adding shade in 3777.
2. Follow with colour 355.
3. Start lightening with colour 918.
4. Follow with some sections filled in with 919.
5. Arm of the couch filled in with 22.
6. Adding orange 3776.
7. Filling the rest of the space in 922
8. Adding wood along the bottom and adding colour 22 over lighter sections.
9. Blending colours throughout couch with colour 22.

Begin the couch with two strands of floss, in Dark Coffee Brown colour 801, using split stitch. Fill in the couch in Very Dark Terra Cotta colour 3777, Dark Terra Cotta colour 355, and Dark Red Copper colour 918, splitting the floss into two strands. Flow in the direction of the couch, to keep the shape of each cushion and, most importantly, the perspective. Each section is satin-stitched with the shadow in the darker shade, colour 3777, fading to the lightest shade, Light Copper colour 922. Embroider with long stitches and, to bend the thread to stay on the curved shapes, use a couch stitch and tack with a tiny tack.

Tone down the lighter sections of the couch by layering with Alizarin colour 22, using a single strand. Stitch over the lighter colours in the direction of the existing stitches, until only a small amount of highlight is showing. Continue with this colour throughout the couch, adding long stitches randomly over the other colours, blending the tones together. Again, go with the direction of stitches already made. Create the wood along the bottom of the couch by using a satin stitch with three strands of floss in colour 801. The highlights on the legs are small touches of Dark Golden Brown colour 975.

Lamp

Begin by filling in the lamp with sections of satin stitch, splitting each floss into three strands. The colour blocking is just a suggestion for how to join the colours together. If you're confident in blending the colours using long and short stitches to make the lamp look more realistic, then the sections are to be used as a guide. The lightest section is Off White colour 746, followed by two sections of Very Light Topaz colour 727. The middle section is filled in with Medium Yellow colour 743 and framed in Dark Straw colour 3820. Couch-stitch the outside of the lamp with the darker shade, with a single strand. The small light detail is in colour 746, along with the satin-stitch lampshade, which is done with one strand of floss. The light section of the lampshade is created with Cream light effect colour E746, split into one strand of floss. Outline the shade with a couch stitch in the same light effect floss.

The small table is satin-stitched with two strands of floss, in Dark Old Gold colour 680, changing the direction of stitches on each small section. Outline in a darker colour, Black Brown colour 3371, with a single strand of floss, using a couch stitch.

1. Blocking the colours together.
2. Adding darker shade to lamp and lighter thread to lampshade.
3. Adding light effect thread.
4. Blocking the colours together and outlining table.

Carpet

1. Larger section of the carpet with chunky French knot.

2. French knot with six strands under furniture.

For the carpet, French knots are used to recreate a shag pile carpet. Place the French knots tightly together to create the texture. It doesn't matter how neat or messy the knots are; it all adds to the effect. You will need two colours: the darker to add shadow under the furniture, Olive Green colour 732, using six strands of floss, and the lighter to fill the rest of the carpet, Light Olive Green colour 734, doubling the floss over to create a chunky twelve-strand knot. Use the doubled floss for the centre of the carpet and reduce into six strands as you get closer to the edge of the furniture, then fade into the darker shade 732.

Pampas Grass

To create these little peeps of pampas grass, each stitch is looped and secured down before creating another loop. A lot of the shape will be lost, but you won't lose the effect of the plant. Start at the tip of each pampas tuft and layer each loop up. Once you've filled these areas with loop stitches, they can then be cut. The pampas grass is made with two colours, Ecru and Light Mocha Brown colour 3782, using all six strands of floss. Add the stems with one long straight stitch.

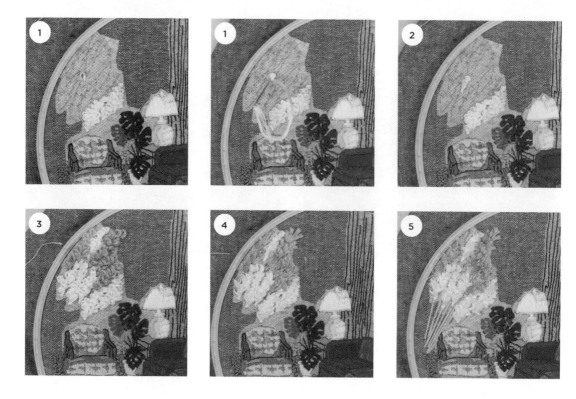

1. Looping thread and securing it to fabric.
2. Layering loops slightly on top of each other.
3. Filling the section, packed tightly.
4. Looped tightly before cutting.
5. Adding stems.

PEACOCK CHAIR

My embroidery journey started with mid-century interiors. I've always been fascinated by the sixties and seventies, especially the way homes were styled—the orange and brown colour palette, the clash of patterns, and the shag pile carpets all mix together to make such an interesting subject to embroider. Here, I've created a beautiful mid-century interior for you to embroider. In this project, I've manipulated the threads to create an unconventional look.

What You Need:

- Eight-inch embroidery hoop or DMC triangle hoop, 26.5 x 26cm
- Cotton or linen fabric

- DMC thread: 310, 355, 434, 729, 780, 782, 783, 801, 890, 975, 987, 3052, 3345, 3348, 3363, 3371, 3856, 4150, E436
- DMC Magic Paper

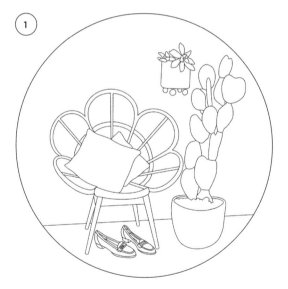

1. Template on page 184.

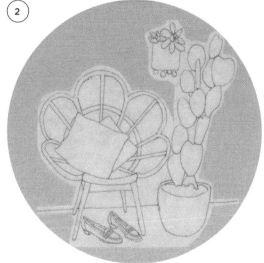

2. Template transferred to Magic Paper and placed on fabric.

I'VE MANIPULATED THE THREADS TO CREATE AN UNCONVENTIONAL LOOK.

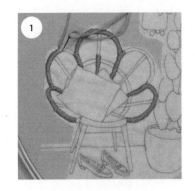

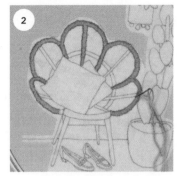

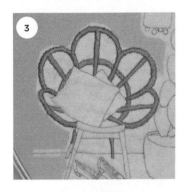

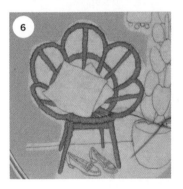

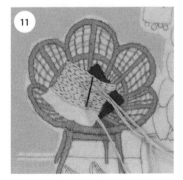

Choose a fabric for the background of this scene and transfer the template onto it. A patterned fabric can give the look of wallpaper, which can add interest. I use DMC Magic Paper to transfer the template. This way you have more control over the placement in the hoop.

Chair

1. Satin-stitching the edges of the chair.
2. Next section split into three strands.
3. Stitch the back legs with two strands.
4. Stitch the front legs with four strands.
5. The last main section is six strands of floss.
6. Straight stitches.
7. Weaving the seat section.
8. Couch-stitch to open spaces.
9. Whipped spider wheel.
10. Weaving two strands.
11. Satin stitch and chain stitch.

Using Medium Topaz colour 783, begin by using a satin stitch, with all six strands of floss, to fill in the chair. Follow the diagram I've provided that indicates the direction of the stitches. Following the shape of the chair, start by stitching the outside with vertical stitches; as you bend around and follow the curve of the chair, your stitches should bend with it and start to become horizontal.

Satin-stitch the two front legs in Medium Old Gold colour 729, splitting the floss into four strands. Continue to the front of the chair with six strands. For the last section of the chair that connects the legs, stitch with two strands of floss with the original colour used to fill in the chair, 783.

The section of the chair that you sit on is filled in with a woven basket stitch. This section is in Dark Topaz colour 782, splitting the floss into three strands. Start by placing separated straight stitches in this small section, then weave in and out of those stitches. Using the same colour, couch-stitch two lines to each open space of the chair. Start with three strands of floss and, as you work up to the top of the chair, reduce to two strands.

With colour 729, split the floss into two strands and add a weave to the couch stitches. The stitch we are going to use is a whipped spider wheel, but inside-out stitch in a circle shape. We are going to use the straight lines like in a basket weave.

I've left the pattern for the cushions blank, so you can fill them in however you wish. You can add a pattern of your choosing to them or use designs from the templates in the book. If you would like to follow the pattern exactly, this is how I've done it. The front cushion is filled in with a chain stitch in Pale Beechwood colour 3856, using all six strands of floss. The back cushion is satin stitch, in Dark Terra Cotta colour 355, again with six strands.

Cactus

Embroider each cactus section using a satin stitch, keeping each stitch as neat and as flat as you can, changing the direction of stitches for each section. The floss is split into two strands for all colours. Going from the darkest to the lightest shade, we are using Ultra Dark Pistachio Green colour 890, Dark Hunter Green colour 3345, Dark Forest Green colour 987, Medium Pine Green colour 3363, and Medium Green Grey colour 3052.

The soil is made up of French knots in Black Brown colour 3371, using all six strands. To create more texture, add two sizes by wrapping the floss around the needle twice for a loose, chunky knot, and once around the needle for a tight, neat knot.

To create the look of the pot, start by adding long stitches vertically, the length of the pot. This is in Ultra Very Dark Topaz colour 780, splitting the floss into three strands. Make sure you leave spaces between the long stitches for weaving. Using the same colour, but with six strands, start to weave in and out of the stitches horizontally. Anchor the thread into the fabric first, before you start to weave. Once you've reached the end of the pot, go back into the fabric and come back through, making a separate hole right next to the previous one. Weave the opposite way. Continue until the pot is full and your basket weave is complete.

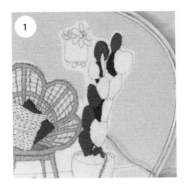

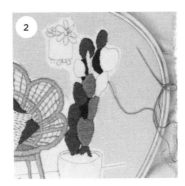

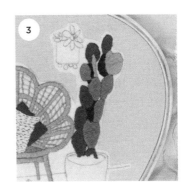

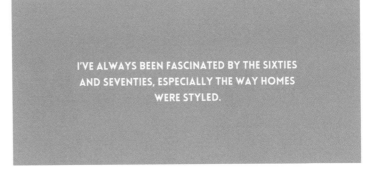

I'VE ALWAYS BEEN FASCINATED BY THE SIXTIES
AND SEVENTIES, ESPECIALLY THE WAY HOMES
WERE STYLED.

1. Start with 890 and 3345.

2. Follow with 987.

3. Finish with the lightest shades 3363 and 3052.

4. French knot soil.

5. Long stitches.

6. Weaving in opposite directions every time.

THE ORANGE AND BROWN COLOUR PALETTE,
THE CLASH OF PATTERNS, AND THE SHAG PILE
CARPETS ALL MIX TOGETHER TO MAKE SUCH AN
INTERESTING SUBJECT TO EMBROIDER.

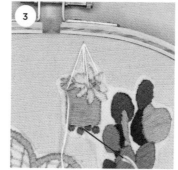

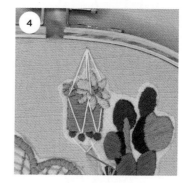

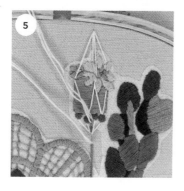

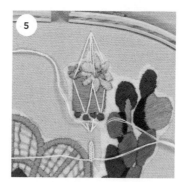

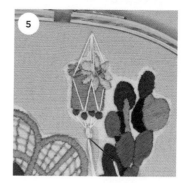

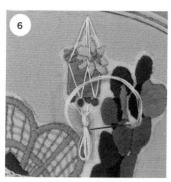

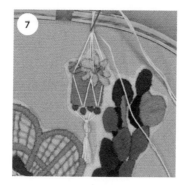

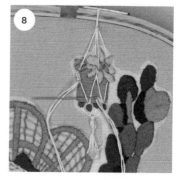

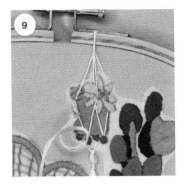 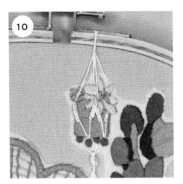 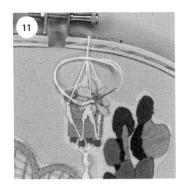

1. Satin-stitched plant.
2. Horizontal satin-stitch pot.
3. Adding long stitches.
4. Four stitches on pot and from beads.
5. Double cast-on stitch.
6. Adding tassel loops.
7. Wrapping around hoop, securing stitches down.
8. Under the long stitch.
9. Create a loop and pull.
10. Build up knots on each long stitch.
11. French knots.

Hanging Plant

Start by satin-stitching each section of the succulent in Light Yellow Green 3348 and Medium Green Grey colour 3052, using all six strands of floss. Satin-stitch the pot in Dark Yellow Beige colour 3045, splitting into three strands. The stitches should be horizontal. Satin-stitch the four balls on the bottom of the pot in colour 780, using all six strands.

To create the macramé, you need to use three strands of floss. With Desert Sand colour 4150, embroider a long stitch from the pot to the very top of the hoop. Stitch as close to the hoop as you can. Repeat three more times. Stitch over the pot in a triangle shape, to the top of the pot and down to the satin-stitched brown beads, as shown; you should have four stitches over the pot. Do the same triangle shapes on the bottom, coming from the beads, and all joining to a point slightly lower down. Working from those joined four stitches, embroider a double cast-on stitch by doubling the strands (back to six strands).

Add a tassel after the cast-on stitch. Create two loops and don't pull them through the fabric. Secure them down on the top, like a messy satin stitch. Then you can cut the loops and trim to desired length.

Going back to the top of the four stitches, join them together by adding a long stitch which wraps around the hoop, and tack them together with small horizontal stitches.

Go back to the stitches over the pot to add some detail. Come through the fabric right at the edge of the pot and go under the long stitch already there, making a loop and pulling tight. Repeat until you build up knots on the stitch. Finish off by stitching a French knot on the top of the long stitch, the hanging string.

Loafers

1. Outline.
2. Adding browns.
3. Darker shade, adding metallic.

I've added a pair of quirky loafers to give a little dimension and add a bit of fun to the piece. First, outline the shoes in Black colour 310, with a single strand of floss, filling in the sole and inside of the shoe. Satin-stitch each tiny section in two strands of floss, starting with Dark Golden Brown colour 975 for the front of the shoe. Follow with the lightest shade, Light Brown colour 434, and the rest is stitched with the darker shade, Dark Coffee Brown colour 801. Fill in the buckle detail with Bronze light effect floss, colour E436, splitting into three strands. Add a long stitch inside the shoe, with one strand.

Floor

Adding French knots to the flooring in colour 4150 variegated floss, Beige Cream.

There are many options you can use to create the floor or carpet. Different stitch techniques will change the look of the embroidery. To create a textured carpet, you can use velvet stitch, French knots, or basket weave to long and short stitches. If you want to carry on the sleek look and try to create a wood floor, you can satin-stitch the large area and stitch over it with a couch stitch in a darker thread.

CHAPTER 7:

DOLLS

NESTING DOLL

Inspired by my daughter's love of nesting dolls, I've created this doll template that can be used in a couple of ways. The doll can be finished with legs and arms, or they can be left off. The pattern can be sized up to create doll-shaped cushions or be embroidered onto clothing. Each doll can be made unique by decorating the body with the floral patterns presented earlier (see pages 181-182 for floral templates that can be used).

What You Need:

- Fabric that doesn't stretch, like cotton, cotton linen, or calico
- DMC embroidery floss
- Tapestry and milliners needles for embroidery work
- In-between needle for stitching together
- Any size embroidery hoop

- Scissors and pinking shears
- Sewing machine with thread (hand-stitching together is okay)
- Thread on a bobbin, in a colour that matches the fabric
- Toy stuffing
- Turning tool

Template on page 185.

Preparing Fabric for Doll

Stitch around the outline with a running stitch.

You'll notice that there are two templates for the doll. There is a rounder doll, and one with cut lines on the body. If you would like to add arms and legs, use the doll pattern with cut lines. If you are just using the body (adding no arms and legs to your doll), then you need to use the other template with the rounder body.

Start by tracing the design onto tracing paper to create a template. Next, place the template on the fabric and trace it using a pen. Then, transfer a floral pattern to the body. Place the fabric inside an embroidery hoop. Don't cut the doll out at this stage. Using a running stitch, stitch around the outline of the doll.

Tip: If you don't have a light box, you can tape the template to a window and set the fabric over it to trace.

Body

1. Attaching face to body and cutting excess fabric.
2. Correct sides together and pin closed.
3. Stitch together leaving a 1.5-inch opening at the bottom.
4. Using the cut lines, larger opening for legs.
5. Turning doll from inside out.
6. Filling doll.
7. Invisible stitch to close the doll.
8. Pulling together to close.

Embroidery designs for the body can be found on pages 181-182.

INSPIRED BY MY DAUGHTER'S LOVE OF NESTING DOLLS, I'VE CREATED THIS DOLL TEMPLATE THAT CAN BE USED IN A COUPLE OF WAYS.

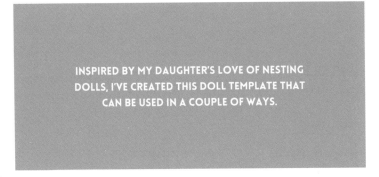

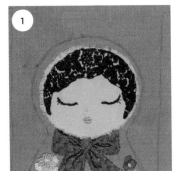

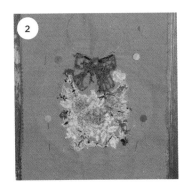

If you embroidered on a separate piece of fabric for the doll's face, this is where it needs stitching to the body. Pin it into place and run around the circle shape on the sewing machine. Keep to the hairline as closely as possible—overlapping is fine. You can also hand-stitch this step, using a back stitch. Once attached, cut away the excess fabric, leaving a small amount to fray.

Once the embroidery you've added to the doll's body is complete, remove the fabric from the hoop. Position a piece of fabric over the front of the doll, making sure the correct side of the fabric is touching the embroidered side. (The correct sides should be facing each other.) Pin the fabric together and stitch along the outline of the doll. Leave an opening of an inch and a half at the bottom. Cut around the doll, leaving a quarter-inch seam, and overlock the edges. If you don't have a sewing machine to stitch the doll together, you can use a running back stitch and pinking shears to stop the edges from fraying.

If you are adding arms and legs, the edge of your doll is the cut line; this means your doll isn't as round. Leave a two-inch opening on the bottom for the legs to slot in.

Turn the doll in the right way through the opening you left and fill it with toy stuffing until you like the shape. You can also use scraps of fabric or wool to give your doll its shape.

To close the hole, fold in the fabric a quarter-inch to create a folded edge, and pin it closed. Next, sew it closed using an invisible stitch. To do so, place the needle into the fold, along the fold and out the same side, then go into the other fold exactly opposite. This will create tiny little stitches that you can pull in tight once you reach the end of the opening.

Before you close it up, you can add bells or a rattle if you would like the doll to make a sound when shaken.

Adding Arms & Legs

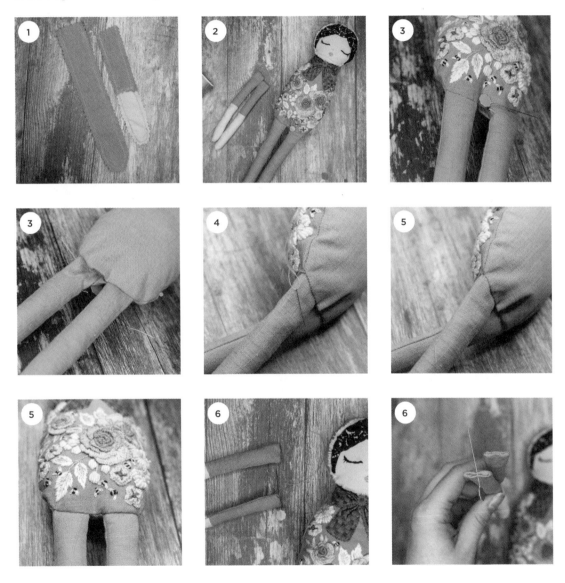

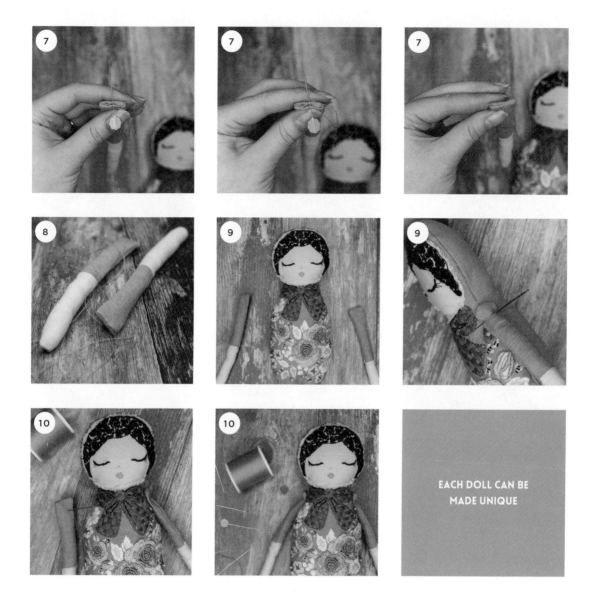

EACH DOLL CAN BE
MADE UNIQUE

1. Stitch together and use pinking shears on edges.
2. Pin legs to body.
3. Invisible stitch to close together.
4. Sewing together.
5. Pulling invisible stitch tight.
6. Folding in the edges and pinning.
7. Using invisible stitch to close.
8. Pulling stitch tight to close.
9. Stitching arms to body.
10. Stitching through to the other side of the doll.

Begin by creating a template for the arms and legs. Place the correct sides together, and pin and stitch them together. Double-stitch for extra security, close to the edge. Instead of overlocking the edges, use pinking shears—this makes it easy when it comes to turning the fabric right-side-out. Don't stitch the top (the flat edge).

Next, turn the pieces right-side-out. You might need to use a turning tool if the arms are thin. Fill the arms and legs with toy stuffing until you are happy with the shape.

Place the legs in the leg openings and pin in place. Hand-stitch the legs to secure them to the doll using an invisible stitch, or, if you prefer, use a sewing machine to close the edge.

Fold in a quarter-inch seam in the tops of the arms and stitch them closed using an invisible stitch. Stitch them to the body with a horizontal stitch that goes through the doll to the other side.

Finishing Touches

Adding blush.

Add colour to the cheeks with a multi-purpose craft ink like Versa Craft. Using a small brush, pat the ink softly onto the brush and add to fabric using circular motions. Set the ink with heat, from either an iron or a heat gun. I've used 132 Apricot, 134 Bubble Gum, and 157 Ash Rose.

NESTING DOLL OPTION 1

What You Need:

- Fabric that doesn't stretch, like cotton, cotton linen, or calico
- DMC embroidery floss: Blanc, 157, 160, 310, 367, 371, 524, 676, 725, 727, 734, 800, 931, 932, 951, 3064 3348, 3855, 4090
- Tapestry and milliners needles for embroidery work
- In-between needle for stitching together
- Any size embroidery hoop
- Scissors and pinking shears
- Sewing machine with thread (hand-stitching together is okay)
- Toy stuffing
- Turning tool

Template on page 185.

Embroidering the Body

Although the patterns for the body are very similar for both dolls, I've simplified the baby doll with more basic embroidery techniques.

Begin by embroidering the bigger leaves using a satin stitch. Split the leaf in the middle to create the look of a vein. Each larger leaf should have two sections of satin stitch. For the leaves, use all six strands in Light Yellow Green colour 3348 and Mustard colour 371. For the stems, use the same colour you are using for the leaves, but with three strands of floss, using a couch stitch.

For the smaller leaves, satin-stitch in one direction in Fern Green colour 524, along with the leaves on the rose buds. For the closed buds, use the same technique in colours 3348 and 524, again using a couch stitch for the stem.

To fill in the three- and four-petal flowers, use a satin stitch, keeping the shape drawn and using six strands of floss for all flowers. The four-petal flowers are stitched in Light Autumn Gold colour 3855, and the three-petal flowers are stitched in 951. The centre of each flower is stitched in Very Light Topaz colour 727.

To create the little bees, embroider tiny stitches for the stripes. Between each yellow stripe of Medium Light Topaz colour 725, embroider a tack stitch in Black colour 310. Finish each little bee with chain-stitched wings using floss divided into two strands in colour Blanc.

Again, using a satin stitch, fill in the small peony flowers in Desert Sand colour 3064. Each petal should be stitched at a slightly different angle to keep the shape of the flower. French-knot the centres of these flowers in Golden Oasis colour 4090. Using the same floss, satin-stitch each tiny centre of the three main roses as well.

The large roses are made up of three shades of blue. Begin with the darkest shade, Medium Grey Blue colour 160. Satin-stitch three sections of the middle flower and five sections on the outer two. Build up the rose with the next shade of blue, Cornflower Blue colour 157. Use a satin stitch on each section around the darker blue. The outer petals of the rose are the lightest shade, Pale Delft Blue colour 800. There is no right or wrong number of sections per colour with these roses, as long as it fades from dark to light. For the rose bud, use a satin stitch in Blue Grey and Light Antique Blue, colours 931 and 932.

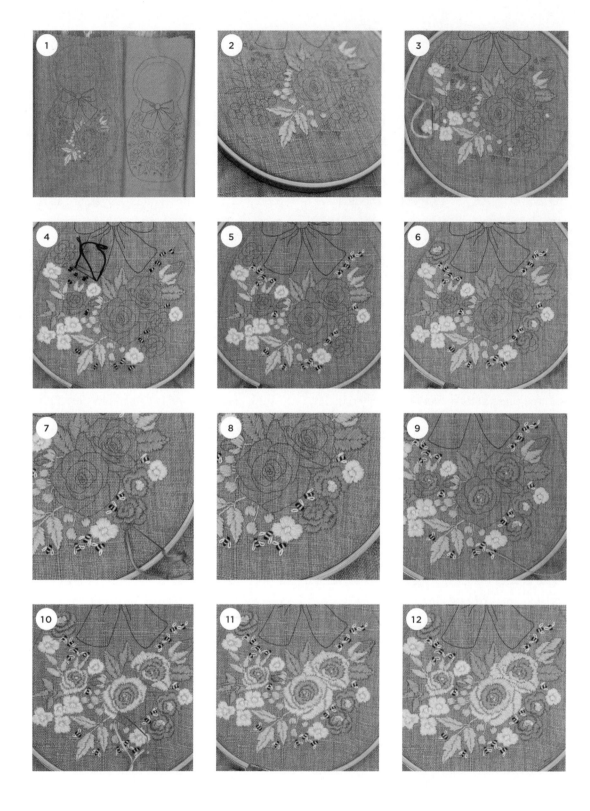

1. Two templates.
2. Leaves stitched with satin stitch and stems with couch stitch.
3. Satin-stitched flowers in 3855 and 951.
4. Yellow and black tack stitches.
5. One chain stitch for each wing.
6. Satin-stitch each petal.
7. Using slightly different angles to keep the shape of the flower.
8. Cluster of French knots in the centre.
9. Darkest shade 160.
10. Medium shade 157.
11. Lightest shade 800.
12. Rose bud.

BOW

 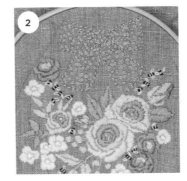 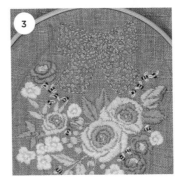

1. Back-stitch the outline.
2. Whipped back stitch and filling with French knots.
3. Adding seed stitch and filling in darker green sections.

Begin by using three strands to outline the bow, using a back stitch in Light Yellow colour 3348. Next, using three strands of floss, turn the back stitch into a whipped back stitch by weaving in and out of the back stitches with Dark Pistachio Green colour 367.

Fill in the bow with scattered French knots in Light Olive Green colour 734. Feel free to stop there, or if you would like to, use a seed stitch to fill in the empty spaces with Mustard colour 371. To make the bow more defined, using three strands of floss, fill in the small details with the darker green you used on the whipped back stitch, colour 367.

Embroidering the Head

FACE

Split-stitch eyes with couch-stitch nose, satin-stitch mouth.

Next, using two strands, create the eyes by using a whipped back stitch along the eye line in Black colour 310. Then, using one strand of floss, embroider tiny stitches to create eyelashes.

In Light Tawny colour 951, split the floss into two strands and then couch-stitch the curved nose. Fill in the lips with a satin stitch in Desert Sand colour 3064, using three strands of floss.

HAIR

In the same colour used on the bow, colour 367, use all six strands of floss to French-knot along the outside of the hair.

Next, whipped-back-stitch along the hairline, using two strands of floss in Light Old Gold colour 676. Leaving a small gap, stitch above the previous line you just stitched, and then repeat. To build up the hair, add more lines of back stitch and then whipped back stitch until the hair is complete.

Note: I have worked the hair colour 676 into the bow, adding seed stitch to the empty spaces.

For the hair, you can follow the Wildflower Floral Template on page 178. The idea is to fill in this section as fully as you can. If you want to use the floral template, here is the mixture of stitches I've used; French knots for the five-point star/flower and couch stitches with tack stitches to create leaves. These stitches are done with all six strands.

To complete the doll, follow the instructions on page 124 from the previous project.

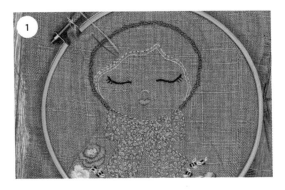
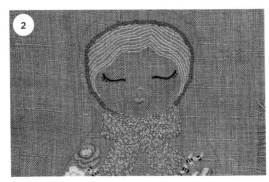

1. Whipped back stitch building up the hair.
2. Adding 676 to bow.

If creating a doll isn't for you, you can also use the doll template to embroider onto clothing or to keep in an embroidery hoop as a piece of art. See the Miniature Nesting Doll Template on page 186.

NESTING DOLL OPTION 2

What You Need:

- Fabric that doesn't stretch, like cotton, cotton linen, or calico
- DMC embroidery floss: Blanc, 224, 225, 310, 434, 451, 452, 453, 676, 819, 3855
- Anchor floss: 1353
- Tapestry and milliners needle for embroidery work
- In-between needle for stitching together
- Any size embroidery hoop
- Scissors and pinking shears
- Sewing machine with thread (hand stitching together is okay)
- Toy stuffing
- Turning tool

Template on page 185.

Transferring to Fabric

For this version of the doll, I've added an applique embroidered face. Trace the doll's facial features onto a separate piece of fabric, leaving out the circle-shaped face but marking it onto the fabric with dots. This will be embroidered and attached before the doll is stitched together. On a sturdier piece of fabric, trace out the doll template and floral pattern. Using a running stitch, go around the edge of the doll.

Embroidering the Body

Start with the bigger leaves and only stitch the middle of each leaf. This is with a variation Anchor floss Mint Green Yellow colour 1353, splitting the floss into three strands and using a mix of long and short stitches to keep the shape of the leaf. Using the same colour, satin-stitch the smaller leaves, splitting the leaf in half with two separate satin-stitched sections to create the look of a vein in the centre. In the same colour, satin-stitch the leaves to the rose buds and couch-stitch each stem, all with the same three strands.

Going back to the six main leaves, continue to fill in the rest of the leaf with long and short stitches, in colour Blanc. Split the floss into three strands to embroider the closed buds using vertical bullion knots. Because you are only using three strands of floss, they won't appear too chunky. Next, couch-stitch each stem.

Fill in the three-petal flowers with a satin stitch, using Light Brown colour 434, with all six strands of floss. For the centre, embroider a chunky French knot, using all six strands and wrapping the floss around the needle two to three times, in Light Medium Gold colour 3855. To create the five remaining flowers, use a cast-on stitch in Light Medium Gold colour 3855, with all six strands of floss. Each petal is a separate cast-on stitch. Twist the floss onto the needle roughly eight to ten times. To fill the empty space, add four straight stitches to create a cross shape and French-knot the centre in colour 434, using all six strands.

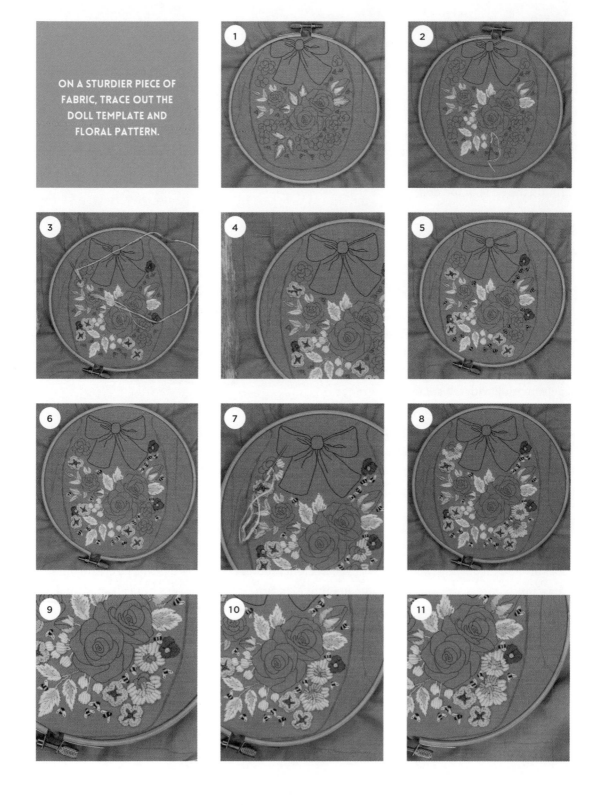

ON A STURDIER PIECE OF FABRIC, TRACE OUT THE DOLL TEMPLATE AND FLORAL PATTERN.

1. Using a variation floss for leaves.
2. Adding white to the leaves and bullion knots to the closed buds.
3. Cast-on stitch for each petal.
4. Straight stitches in brown.
5. Yellow and black tack stitches.
6. One chain stitch for each wing.
7. Outer petals in the lightest shade of pink.
8. One to two sections in medium shade.
9. Filling in the small sections in the darkest shade.
10. Flower built up of bullion knots.
11. Satin-stitch the centre.

To create the little bees, embroider tiny straight stitches for the stripes. Between each yellow stripe of Medium Light Topaz colour 725, embroider a tiny stitch in Black colour 310. Finish each little bee by splitting the floss into two strands and chain-stitching the wings in colour Blanc.

Adding texture to the small peony flowers is done with sections of bullion knots, in various shades of pink, starting with the lightest colour, Light Baby Pink 819, and using all six strands. Each bullion knot has roughly six to eight wraps around the needle. The smaller sections—especially the ends—should be wrapped four times. This may vary, depending upon how raised you want your stitches to be and how thick your needle is.

You should now have four to five petals on each flower filled in with colour 819. To add more drama, add Pink colour 225, onto two sections of each flower and one section on one flower. Stitch the last small sections with the darkest shade, Very Light Shell Pink colour 224. Fill in the centres of the flowers with a satin stitch in colour 3855.

FILLING IN THE ROSE

These roses are created using all six strands of floss. Starting with the rose bud, stitch a bullion knot vertically with the lightest shade, Light Shell Grey colour 453. Fill in the other side of the larger rose bud with the next shade, Medium Shell Grey colour 452. The small bud only has a small section of Medium Shell Grey, with the other side filled in with the darkest shade, Dark Shell Grey colour 451.

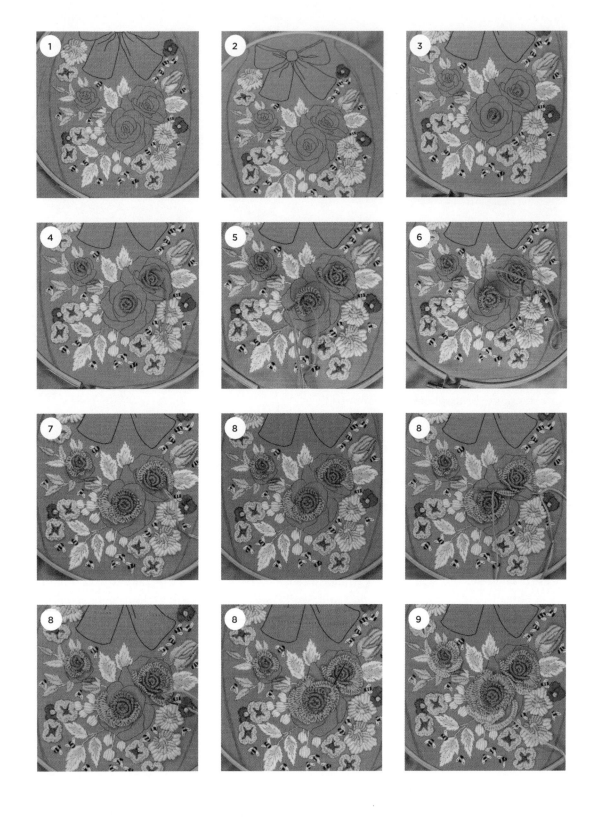

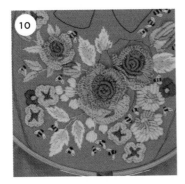

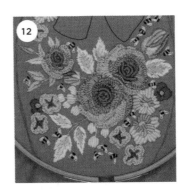

1. Bullion knot with 453.

2. Following with 452, 451.

3. French and bullion knot centres.

4. Bullion-knot the small sections.

5. Cast-on stitch.

6. Using straight stitches to fill in gaps.

7. Cast-on stitch sitting at the top of the petal.

8. Stitching in between the long sections of the cast-on stitch.

9. Cast-on stitch in 453.

10. Longer stitches to fill in gaps.

11. Holding the petal shape with a tack.

12. Using 452 to break the roses up.

Next, beginning with the darkest shade first, colour 451, stitch a French knot in the very centre, followed by a bullion knot around it. Follow the template to see where each knot should start and finish. Fill the small sections of the rose with bullion knots.

As the petal shape widens, larger stitches are needed to fill each section. Use a cast-on stitch, making sure the top of the stitch is at the top of each petal. You'll notice that there will be a gap to the bottom of the stitch, so use a straight stitch between each little twist created within the cast-on stitch. For the very small section on the right-hand side of the rose, satin-stitch this section.

Once you've gone around the middle of the rose in one colour, you can do the same with the lighter shade. Use colour 452 to build the next layer of the rose, again making sure the top of the cast-on stitch sits against the top of the petal. Fill three to four petals with colour 452 to cover around the darker shade 451.

Next, use the lightest shade, 453, to fill each petal shape. You'll notice these petals are much larger, and therefore the straight stitches need to be longer. To stop the cast-on stitches from moving and to hold the shape of the rose, secure them from the top of the cast-on stitch. For the middle rose, fill in the middle petal with shade 452 to visually break up the roses.

BOW

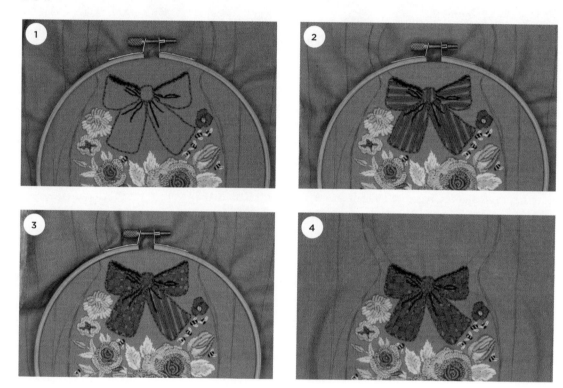

1. Outlining the bow and adding detail in black.
2. Long stitches grouped in three.
3. Creating a basket weave.
4. Weaving horizontally in groups of three.

To begin, use three strands of floss to outline the bow with a back stitch in Light Brown colour 434. Next, again using three strands of floss, satin-stitch the top of the bow in Black colour 310. Add the detail to the bow with the same floss, using a couch stitch.

Create a basket-weave effect to fill the rest of the bow by stitching three long vertical stitches together, leaving a gap of the same width. Repeat the same three stitches until the bow is full. Then, use horizontal stitches to weave the floss in and out of the grouped vertical stitches, also in groups of three. Repeat the process until the bow is filled.

Embroidering the Head

FACE

Next, using two strands, create the eyes by using a whipped back stitch along the eye line in Black colour 310. Then, using one strand of floss, embroider tiny tack stitches to create eyelashes.

In Light Tawny colour 951, split the floss into two strands and then couch-stitch the curved nose. Fill in the lips with a satin stitch in Desert Sand colour, 3064, using three strands of floss, splitting the top and bottom lip.

HAIR

Creating the face and hair.

To create the hair, I've used the Wildflower Floral Template on page 178, filling in the pattern with Black colour 310 and using mostly satin stitch and French knots. Outline the hair with one strand of floss, using a couch stitch.

Don't forget to follow this stitching guide and embroider the flower details on the legs.

NESTING DOLL VARIATIONS

Left: Doll 1; Right: Doll 2.

Here are some possible variations if you would like to mix and match doll patterns.

Doll 1: Large Rose and Bees

Split-stitch the hair in Very Light Terra Cotta colour 758, with all six strands.

Frame the hair with a line of French knots in Light Baby Pink colour 819, using all six strands. Follow with whipped back stitch, using three strands, in the same colour. French-knot around again with colour variation thread, Morning Meadow colour 4065, using all six strands.

To create the bow, begin by outlining it with a whipped back stitch in Salmon colour 760. Split the floss into three strands. Back-stitch with three strands and "whip" it with the same three strands. Fill in the bow with a five-point-star stitch to create a flower in Light Baby Pink colour 819, using all six strands. Scatter French knots in between with Morning Meadow colour 4065, using all six strands.

I've used the Large Rose Template on page 179 to create the design on the body and have used all six strands of floss for this design. The rose is built up with a French-knot centre in colour 758, then bullion knots stitched around in the same colour, and finished off with cast-on stitch in colour 819. Stitch the leaves with a leaf stitch in colour 524 and 3013. Then, whipped-back-stitch the stems with two strands of floss. To create the three flowers, French-knot the centres in colours 801 and 436, with the petals made up of long and short stitches in colours 3774, 3856, and 712. Finish the design by adding tiny bees, using tiny straight stitches for each stripe, in colours 783 and 310. The wings are single chain-stitch using three strands of floss, in Light Baby Pink colour 819.

Doll 2: Small Roses and Scattered Flowers

To create the hair for this doll, use a whipped back stitch in colour 758. Using all six strands of floss, begin at the edge where the hair frames the face, and stitch the outline. Follow the same shape for each line. To frame the hair with this frill, use a cast-on stitch in colour Blanc, using all six strands of floss. These cast-on stitches are made up of six stitches, so you should have roughly twenty-three cast-on stitches around the head.

The bow is outlined with whipped back stitch in Morning Meadow colour 4065, using all six strands of floss. Fill in the empty space with fat French knots, doubling the floss and knotting with twelve strands in Very Light Fern Green colour 524. Add seed stitches at random in Light Yellow Green colour 3348, using six strands.

I've used a template (the Small Rose Template, seen on page 180) for the doll's body design. To make the rose, French-knot the centre in colour 221, framing it with bullion knots. Then build up the rose with cast-on stitches, first with colour 754 and then colour 3774. The smaller rose has French knots in the centre in Blanc and is built up with cast-on stitch in colour 754. Stitch the leaves with a leaf stitch, using all six strands, in colours 3348 and 3053. Using the same colour, split the floss into three strands and then whipped-back-stitch the stem. The three clustered flowers have French knots in the centres in colour 3348, with the petals built around in cast-on stitch colour Blanc. Again, use all six strands of floss. I've added French knots in the empty space with twelve strands, to pull the white in and to mimic the design on the bow.

Doll 3: Doll with Legs

For the hair, I've traced a section of the template from the floral bee pattern (on pages 179-180), following the stitch guide to this floral embroidery. Stitch with colour 842, using all six strands. The hair is framed with French knots in colour 4145, again using six strands. The second-layer French knots are scattered in colour 503, splitting the floss into three strands.

The bow shape is outlined with colour 3772, stitching with whipped back stitch, using two strands. Also outline the bottom of the face. Fill in the bow with French knots, in all six strands of floss. The pink shades you'll need are colours 224, 754, 758, 760, 761, and 3779. Highlight with tiny stitches in colour (green) and colour (green).

For the design on the body, I've used the pincushion template on page 177.

Rose 1: French-knot the centre in colour 3859, then follow the template around with a bullion knot. Keep building up the petals with cast-on stitch in colour 758, and the outer petals in colour 754.

Rose 2: French-knot the centre in colour 760, bullion-knot around, then use cast-on stitch to keep building the rose up in the same colour. Continue with colour 761, then to colour 224 on the outer petals. Leaf-stitch the leaves in colours 524 and 503. Satin-stitch the rest of the leaves in colour 4145.

The stems are couch-stitch with three strands of colour 524.

For the flowers, French-knot the centres in colour 746. The petals are created with bullion knot in colours 739 and 3033.

The lavender is lots of French knots grouped together in colours 05, 06, and 451. The French knots in the centre are in colour 3774.

This doll has font added, from pages 188-189. The name is satin-stitched in three strands of floss, in colour 4145. More information about stitching fonts can be found on page 161.

BEE DOLL

I wanted to create a whimsical project for you to practice creating texture that is also beautiful. I love bees, so an idea quickly took shape. The project could involve embroidering blocks of the bee's yellow and black stripes with florals. I've created a simple bee shape that can be sized up and made into a cushion, kept at the standard size to make into a cuddly toy, or sized down into a coin purse. The project is versatile—it can be a doll, a purse, or simply a piece of art.

What You Need:

- · Mustard-coloured linen cotton or natural calico
- · Milliners needle, in-between needle
- · DMC embroidery floss: Blanc, Ecru, 310, C310, 676, 728, 729, 743, 782
- · Scissors and pinking shears
- · Sewing machine and thread
- · Any size embroidery hoop
- · Toy stuffing

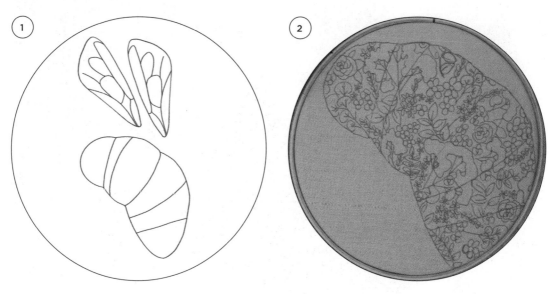

1. Template on page 187.

2. Template traced onto matieral.

How-To:

1. Trace the bee body and florals onto fabric. 2. Place the fabric in the hoop.

Trace the bee template onto tracing paper and then cut out the shape. Lay the template on the fabric and then transfer it onto the fabric. Alternatively, if you prefer, you can freehand-draw the body shape onto the fabric, rather than using the template. I like to do that when I want a larger piece of fabric to work on. When I draw patterns onto fabric freehand, I used a heat pen, which works well.

You will also need the Wildflower Floral Pattern Template to fill the inside of the bee (find it on page 178). Lay your fabric over the floral design and trace straight onto fabric. Continue the drawing until the whole body is covered. Then place the fabric in an embroidery hoop, keeping the fabric taut.

COLOUR KEY FOR BEE STRIPES

- First section: Black 310 and C310
- Second section: 743, 728, 782
- Third section: Black 310 and C310
- Forth section: 782, 729, 728, 743
- Fifth section: Black 310 and C310
- Sixth: 743, 676, Ecru, Blanc

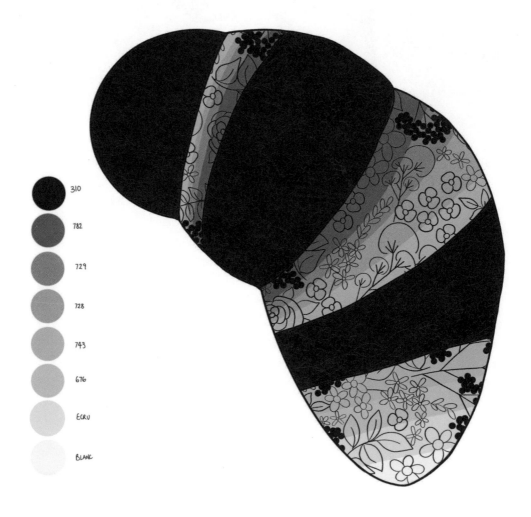

310

782

729

728

743

676

ECRU

BLANC

FLOWER STITCHING CHART

Elderflower: Five-point flower in open sections with three strands, couch-stitch with two strands for stem.

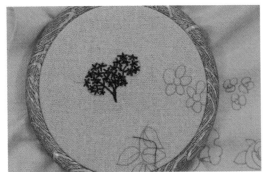

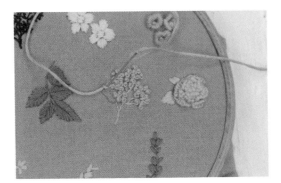

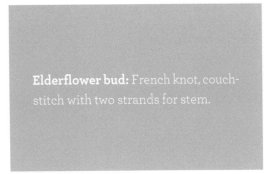

Elderflower bud: French knot, couch-stitch with two strands for stem.

Leaf: Satin-stitch two halves of leaf with three strands. Couch-stitch stem with two strands and one strand to secure.

Three-petal flowers: Bullion knot, French knot centre, using all six strands.

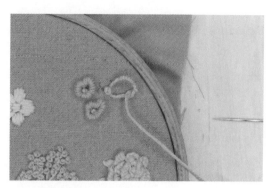

Rose: French knot centre. For the shapes surrounding the French knot, you need to use a bullion knot around it, followed by cast-on stitch on edges. These roses are created using all six strands of floss.

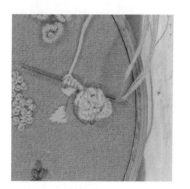
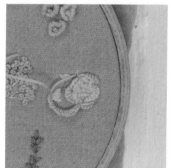

Tiny flowers: A mix of five-point flowers, one straight stitch for each petal, that join from the centre and granitos-stitch each petal, also joining from the centre. The granitos stitch creates a chunky flower, so use this method where you have more space to fill instead of the delicate stitches.

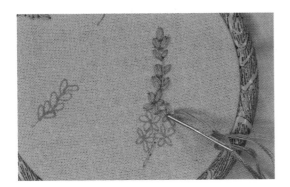

Tiny flowers on branch: Granitos-stitch each five-point flower, joining in the middle. Granitos-stitch on each bud, using all six strands. Couch-stitch the stem with two strands and one strand to secure.

Larger flowers: Satin-stitch each petal and centre.

Embroider Floral Design

ADDING BLACK STRIPES

Using six strands in Black colour 310, start filling in the design; the sections that need to be black are one, three, and four. Fill in the black sections as fully as you can, trying to cover most of the fabric. After following the floral design, you can go back in and fill the gaps with five-point flowers and French knots. It will just add to the wildflower feel. Use C310 to add a little sparkle to the matte black for contrast. I've embroidered most all the design in Black 310 and used C310 sparkle for the bullion-knot flowers and the five-point flowers on elderflower, then filled in the gaps with the same flower. This is stitched with three strands of floss.

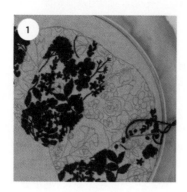 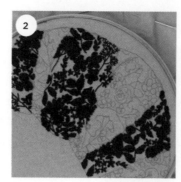 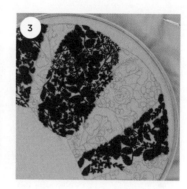

1.   Filling in black stripes.
2.   Adding black sparkle.
3.   Filling in the gaps with tiny flowers.

ADDING YELLOW STRIPES

Using six strands, fade in colours Medium Yellow 743, Topaz 728, Medium Old Gold 729, and Dark Topaz 782 in the second section, working from the lightest shade to the darkest. In section 4, start with the darkest shade and work back to the lightest, in colours Dark Topaz 782, Medium Old Gold 729, Topaz 728, and Medium Yellow 743.

Section 6 is a little lighter than the other two stripes, starting with colour Medium Yellow 743, stitching a small amount closest to the black stripe, fading to Light Old Gold 676, then to Ecru, and finishing with Blanc at the tip.

I WANTED TO CREATE A WHIMSICAL PROJECT FOR
YOU TO PRACTICE CREATING TEXTURE THAT IS
ALSO BEAUTIFUL.

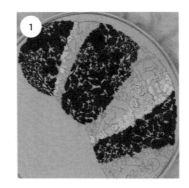

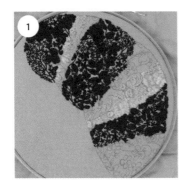

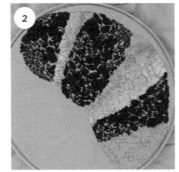

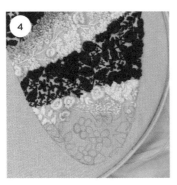

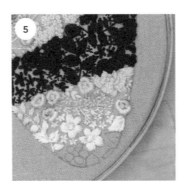

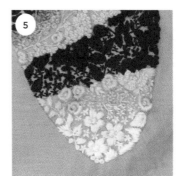

1. Using 743 and 728
2. Using 729.
3. Using 782.
4. Using 743, 676.
5. Using Ecru.

MAKING THE WINGS

1. Tracing the floral design onto wings.

2. Weaving the back stitch to create a whipped back stitch.

To create the wings, you need a light-coloured fabric. I've opted for natural calico. Trace the bee template onto the fabric. Embroider along the veins with a whipped back stitch in Ecru. Split the floss into three strands and start with a back stitch. Only stitch the pattern inside the wings, not the outline. Once all the edges are filled, start weaving the thread in and out of the back stitch to create a whipped back stitch.

I've added tiny floral accents to the edges of the wings, using the same floral template to fill in the bee. Trace a small amount to the wings. Fill this section to your preference. I've embroidered a small satin-stitched flower, a bullion-knot flower, French knots scattered, and five-point flowers.

Bee Taking Shape

Once the embroidery is complete, trace the outline of the bee template on the reverse side, then set a piece of fabric over the front with the right side facing the embroidered side and pin into place. Sew the two pieces together, leaving an inch open on the body so you can add stuffing. Overlock the edges for extra security, but you can also trim the edges with pinking shears.

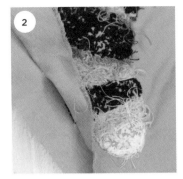

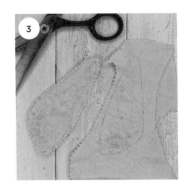

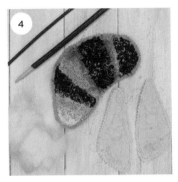

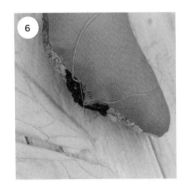

KEEP AT THE STANDARD SIZE TO MAKE INTO A CUDDLY TOY, OR SIZE DOWN INTO A COIN PURSE.

1. Sewing bee together on reverse side.
2. Opening left for stuffing.
3. Sewing wings together and pinking the edges.
4. Turning bee and wings in right way.
5. Stuffing bee.
6. Invisible stitch to close the bee.
7. Invisible stitch to close the wings.
8. Sewing the wings onto the bee with shorter corners touching.

Turn the bee right-side-out, and through the little opening, fill the cavity with toy stuffing until it is as full as you like.

To close the hole, fold in a quarter-inch of fabric to create a folded edge and pin the fabric closed. Next, stitch the folded edge with an invisible stitch by inserting the needle into the fold, along it for a quarter-inch and out the same side, then going into the other fold exactly opposite. You'll create tiny stitches that you can pull in tight, once you reach the end of the opening. Stitch the wings onto the bee with the same thread you closed up the wings with. Position one on the plain fabric, onto the back of the bee, and the other into the middle black stritpe.

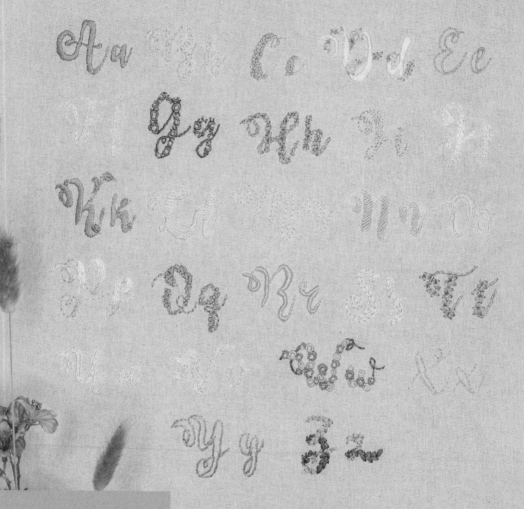

FONT

When it comes to embroidering letters, it is tempting to use a lot of floss, but using fewer strands will give you more control because you can keep the floss tight to the fabric and gradually build up the stitches. There is no right or wrong way to do it, and the creative possibilities are endless.

When transferring font to fabric, the easiest method to use is water-soluble fabric, rather than drawing straight onto the fabric, which will show at the end (unless you use a pen that will disappear).

Letter A

Satin stitch A.

Filling in the letters with a satin stitch is the most effective. It's clean and easily built up for an embossed look. I use three strands of floss and stitch on a slight diagonal. As you are stitching, you'll notice that, as you bend around the curves of the letter, the direction of your stitches will change slightly. The smaller details can be filled in with a whipped back stitch or a couch stitch. This allows you to manipulate the thread into the curved shape.

Letters B & C

Try filling in the larger areas with florals or French knots. It doesn't matter if you have gaps, as long as you have stitched to the line of the letter so you keep the shape intact. Fill in the small details with whipped back stitch, back stitch, or couch stitch.

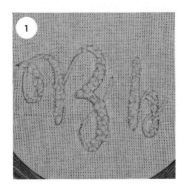

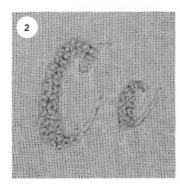

1. Filling with granitos flowers.

2. Filling with French knots.

Letter D

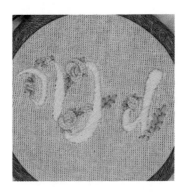

Decorating with cast-on roses and satin stitch.

You can add little embellishments to the letters, decorating the line work with cast-on roses and tiny leaf details. Stitch with three strands of floss to keep the roses small enough to keep the shape of the D. After you've made your creative additions, fill in the rest of the letter with the same techniques used in letter A, using satin stitch to fill in the larger sections and whipped back stitch for the line work.

Letters E & F

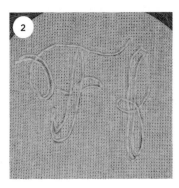

1. Outline with whipped back stitch.
2. Outline with couch stitch.

Keep the letter hollow by outlining it with back stitch, whipped back stitch, couch stitch, stem stitch, or split stitch. Continue to use the same stitch on the thin details. Make sure the stitches are smaller as you curve and loop around. The letters are outlined with three strands of floss.

Letter G

Filling with bullion-knot flowers.

Fill in the letter with three-dimensional flowers, using a bullion knot and French knot centres to create tiny three-petalled flowers. Embroider these flowers in the larger spaces of the letter, then use a whipped back stitch to fill in the thinner sections, the line work. I also add greenery to the flowers to help fill in the gaps and to fill in the letter's shape. The bullion flowers are embroidered with all six strands of floss.

Letter H

French knots, five-point flowers, and seed stitches.

Use a mix of French knots, five-point flowers, and seed stitches to fill the entire letter, reducing the amount of embroidery you add to the thinner part of the letter. The chunky embroidery is created with six strands of floss.

Letters I & J

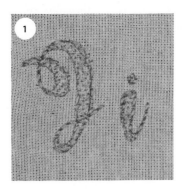
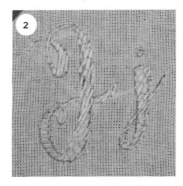

1.   Seed stitch.
2.   Filling with couch stitch.

Another embroidery technique you can use as a filling stitch is seed stitches, layering the stitches on top of each other or stitching just enough to keep the shape of the letter. I've embroidered the I using three strands of floss. Couch stitches can be used tightly packed together or with small gaps in between, stitched on a diagonal with three strands and securing the long stitches with one strand of floss.

Letter K

Adding tiny florals.

Add tiny details to the smallest part of the letter, creating a string of florals. Embroider small cast-on roses with three strands of floss, with French knots, five-point flowers, and tiny stitches for greenery. Fill in the larger sections of the letter with satin stitch.

Letter L

Filling with a weave stitch.

Weave the inside of the letter with a basket stitch on the larger areas. Fill in the line work with whipped back stitch. To create the tiny weave, three strands of floss are used.

Letter M

Outlining with back stitch.

Outline with a back stitch, keeping the straight stitches small to be able to curve around the shape of the letter. Again, use three strands of floss.

Letter N

Filling with bullion knots.

Add texture to the letter N with bullion knots, stitching on a diagonal. Use only three strands to keep the bullion knots small and thinner than normal, and embroider them tightly packed together.

Letter O

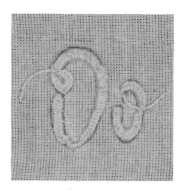

Cast-on-stitched O.

Give the letter a bit more form with a textured stitch, cast-on stitch, embroidering with three strands to keep the cast-on stitch dainty. Make sure the length of the cast-on stitch is the same size as the section you're filling. Secure the stitches down with a tiny stitch to hold the shape of the letter. The capital O is made up of three cast-on stitches, and the line work is filled in with a whipped back stitch.

Letter P

Filling with long and short stitches.

Fill in the letter with long and short stitches, packing the stitches tightly together. Embroider vertically until parts of the letter go into the line work, which is stitched with a back stitch. Embroider with three strands of floss.

Letter Q

French knots and seed stitches.

Embroider with six strands of floss to create chunky French knots in two different colours. Leave gaps as you embroider to add in random seed stitches, a way to add in some greenery. Continue with the thickness of the letter, adding chunky back stitches to the line work.

Letter R

Filling with bullion knots.

Make the letter raised with bullion knots, embroidering each section of the letter with a bullion knot, bending and twisting it to the shape of the letter. The capital R is made up of four bullion knots, stitched into place to hold its shape. The small details are embroidered with couch stitch. This letter is embroidered with all six strands of floss.

Letter S

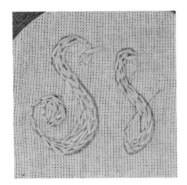

Filling with chain stitch.

Use a chain stitch as a filling stitch. Split the floss into three strands to have more control over each chain stitch, and keep them smaller to be able to curve around the S. The line work is embroidered with back stitch.

Letter T

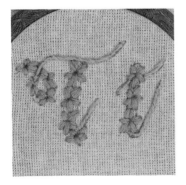

Filling with bullion knots.

Create large flowers with five granitos stitches embroidered together. Use six strands for chunky florals, not filling the entire shape of the letter, but stitching the flowers close together to hold the shape of the letter. Fill in the line work with whipped back stitch, again with six strands.

Letters U & V

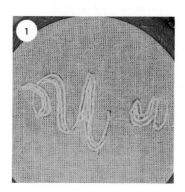 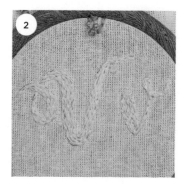

1. Filling with whipped back stitch.
2. Filling with split stitch.

Fill the letter with a stitch you would typically use for outlining. U is created with whipped back stitch, first outlined and then a line of whipped back stitch inside. V is created with split stitch, which is quite an effective filling stitch when packed together tightly. Both letters are stitched with three strands of floss.

Letter W

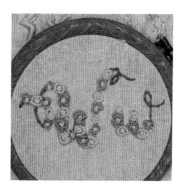

Tiny cast-on and bullion-knot flowers.

Use cast-on stitch and bullion knots to create little flowers. Embroider two stitches together with a French knot centre to create these flowers. Place each flower close to the last. Stitch with three strands of floss. The line work of the W is with couch stitch, using six strands of floss.

Letters X & Y

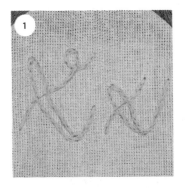
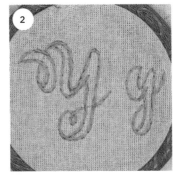

1. Outlined in split stitch.
2. Outlined in stem stitch.

Outline the letters with split stitch and stem stitch, both with three strands of floss.

Letter Z

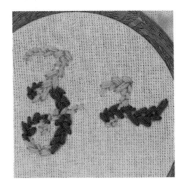

Granitos-stitched leaves.

Granitos stitch can be manipulated in other ways. For the letter Z, I have used a series of granitos stitches, barely touching, to create a vine of leaves.

CHAPTER 9:

TEMPLATES

Mountain

Lavender Field

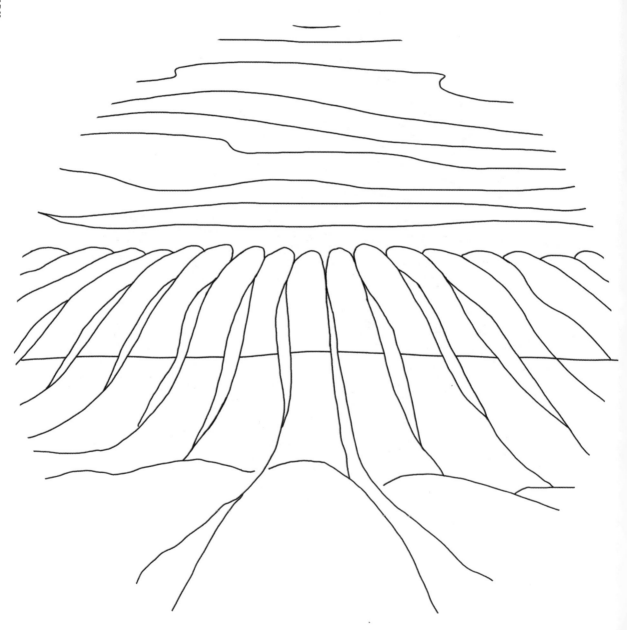

Girl With Ribbon

Girl Hidden behind Flowers

Portrait

Drawstring Bag

Pincushion

Wildflower Pattern Pt 1

Wildflower Pattern Pt 2

Big Rose Pattern Pt 1

Big Rose Pattern Pt 2

Large Rose Pattern Pt 3

Small Rose Pattern

Floral 1

Floral 2

Floral 3

Floral 4

Mid-Century Living

Peacock Chair

Nesting Doll

Nesting Doll with
Arms & Legs

Arms   Legs

Miniature Dolls

Bee

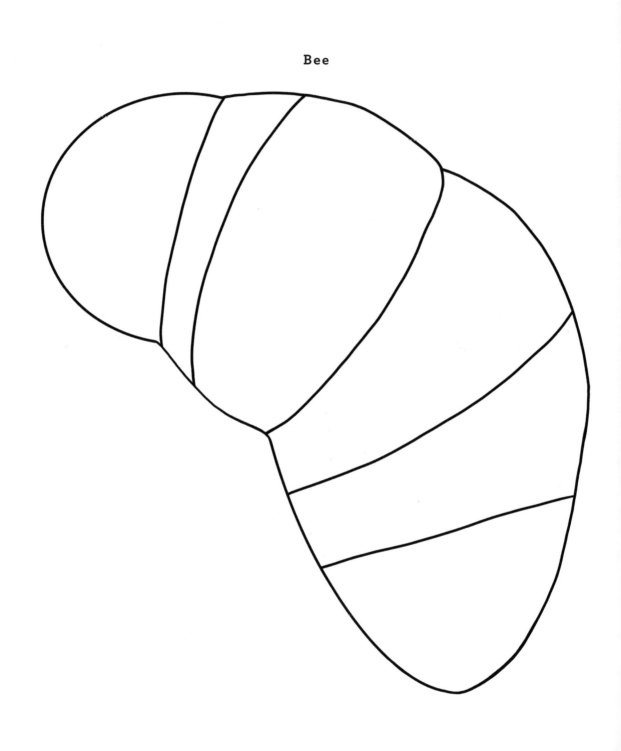

Bee Wings

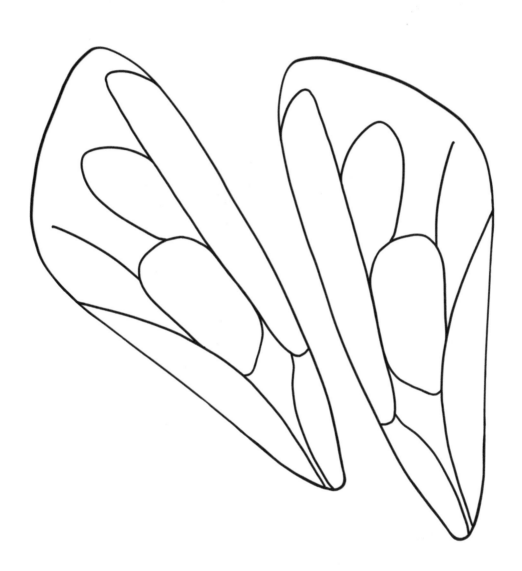

Aa Bb

Ee Ff

Ii Jj

Mm Nn

C c D d

G g H h

K k L l

O o P p

Qq Rr

Uu Vv

Xx Yy

Ss Tt

Ww

Zz

ACKNOWLEDGMENTS

To my mother, who always encouraged creativity, from setting up many craft days with me as a child, to always making beautiful clothes for my dolls. My biggest critic and cheerleader all in one. The one person who wants everything I create displayed in her home.

To my partner John, who understands how important art and creativity are to me, who supports me in every way he can.

My dear friend Aïcha, whose taste level I value the most. The one person I can depend on for her true opinion. The person who always offers her help and support in everything I do, a true friend.

To my very patient editor Lisa, thank you for being so supportive and believing that I could make something I would be proud of.

To all my Instagram followers, the ones who came for the embroidery but stayed for the home life updates. The ones who bought my art at the very start of the road. Thank you for all the support, without you this book wouldn't have been possible.

ABOUT THE AUTHOR

Rachael Dobbins started the Used Threads Instagram as a creative outlet, somewhere she could document her progress and get into the swing of embroidering again, originally getting its name from gifted vintage cotton strands and threads, a collection of beautiful treasures from different eras. She stitches a range of things—from retro mid-century interiors and accessories to thread-painted landscapes and seascapes, from quirky 3D stitches that flow from the hoop to embroidered seventies-inspired clothing.

Stitching from a very young age, Rachael followed in the steps of her grandmother. After going down the fine art route and teaching herself to stitch, Rachael realized that embroidery was her main passion and graduated with a BA honours in textiles and surface design. Now combining both arts, Rachael likes to think that she pushes the boundaries of embroidery, treating the thread strands like strokes of paint on a canvas.

yellow pear 🍐 press

Yellow Pear Press, established in 2015, publishes inspiring, charming, clever, distinctive, playful, imaginative, beautifully designed lifestyle books, cookbooks, literary fiction, notecards, and journals with a certain *joie de vivre* in both content and style. Yellow Pear Press books have been honored by the Independent Publisher Book (IPPY) Awards, National Indie Excellence Awards, Independent Press Awards, and International Book Awards. Reviews of our titles have appeared in Kirkus Reviews, Foreword Reviews, Booklist, Midwest Book Review, San Francisco Chronicle, and New York Journal of Books, among others. Yellow Pear Press joined forces with Mango Publishing in 2020, with the vision to continue publishing clever and innovative books. The fact that they're both named after fruit is a total coincidence.

We love hearing from our readers, so please stay in touch with us and follow us at:

Facebook: Mango Publishing
Twitter: @MangoPublishing
Instagram: @MangoPublishing
LinkedIn: Mango Publishing
Pinterest: Mango Publishing
Newsletter: mangopublishinggroup.com/newsletter